C1190894287

Limitations of Expert Evidence

Based on a conference organised by the Royal College of Physicans and the Royal College of Pathologists

Edited by

Stephen Leadbeatter MB ChB MRCPath

Wales Institute of Forensic Medicine,
University of Wales College of Medicine

The Royal College
of Physicians

The Royal College
of Pathologists

1996

Royal College of Physicians of London
11 St Andrews Place, London NW1 4LE
Registered Charity No 210508

ISBN 1 86016 029 8

Designed and typeset by the Royal College of Physicians Publications Unit

Printed in Great Britain by Cathedral Print Services Ltd, Salisbury

Foreword

With the growing tendency for patients to sue for compensation if something turns out to be less perfect than they expected, more doctors are likely to find themselves in Court to give expert evidence. Doctors are quite accustomed to being asked for, and to give, an instant opinion on almost anything — the dangers of eating beef, the risks of electromagnetic radiation, the causes of obesity, the safe limits of drinking alcohol. But they are often not so good at presenting the evidence on which they base their opinions. This may be because they lack the knowledge and experience expected of an expert witness, but more often because they are poor at presenting the evidence in a manner that can be readily understood by the intelligent lay person and the proverbial man on the Clapham omnibus. As the outcome of a legal action is strongly affected by the manner in which the expert witness — from whatever specialty — presents the evidence before a judge and jury, it is necessary for lawyers and doctors to come together to set out their procedural requirements and obligations and to indicate the constraints placed upon them by circumstances and ethical considerations for gathering the necessary evidence.

The conference, arranged jointly by our two Colleges and on which this book is based, provided a forum for doctors and lawyers to learn from one another where the limitations of expert evidence lie at present and what is needed to progress beyond these boundaries.

L A TURNBERG
President, Royal College of Physicians of London

A J BELLINGHAM
President, Royal College of Pathologists

March 1996

Contributors

Graham Cooke
*Barrister specialising in criminal work, Chambers of Michael Lawson QC,
36 Essex Street, London WC2R 3AS*

Jennifer Cummin
Solicitor, Clyde & Co, 51 Eastcheap, London EC3M 1JP

Nigel LG Eastman MB BSc MRCPsych
*Barrister at Law and Head of Section of Forensic Psychiatry,
St George's Hospital Medical School, Jenner Wing, Cranmer Terrace,
London SW17 ORE*

Roger C Evans MB FRCP
*Consultant in Emergency Medicine, The Accident Unit, Cardiff Royal Infirmary,
Newport Road, Cardiff CF2 1SZ*

David J Gee CBE MB BS FRCPath DMJ
*Emeritus Professor of Forensic Medicine, 27 Boroughbridge Road, Knaresborough,
North Yorkshire HG5 OLY*

Bernard H Knight CBE MD MRCP FRCPath DMJ
*Professor of Forensic Pathology, Wales Institute of Forensic Medicine,
University of Wales College of Medicine, Cardiff Royal Infirmary, Newport Road,
Cardiff CF2 1SZ*

Stephen Leadbeatter MB ChB MRCPath
*Senior Lecturer in Forensic Pathology, Wales Institute of Forensic Medicine,
University of Wales College of Medicine, Institute of Pathology,
Cardiff Royal Infirmary, Newport Road, Cardiff CF2 1SZ*

Patrick J Lincoln PhD MRCPath
*Reader in Haemogenetics, The London Hospital Medical College,
Turner Street, London E1 2AD*

Trevor J Rothwell PhD
*Secretary, Home Office Policy Advisory Board for Forensic Pathology,
Dragons, Cotterstock, Peterborough PE8 5HD*

His Honour Judge Martin Stephens QC MA
Resident Judge, Swansea Crown Court, St Helens Road, Swansea SA1 4PS

David K Whittaker PhD FDSRCS
*Reader in Oral Biology and Consultant, Department of Basic Dental Science,
Dental School, University of Wales College of Medicine, Heath Park, Cardiff CF4 4XY*

Contents

Editor's introduction

This publication brings together papers presented at the conference 'Limitations of expert evidence' on 25 October 1994, organised jointly by the Royal Colleges of Pathologists and Physicians. Personal experience within the criminal courts had raised the question, 'What is it that makes my opinion on these pathological findings such-and-such?', and the occasional corollary question, 'What is it about these pathological findings that makes that expert's opinion different?'. The conference was organised in an attempt to explore these questions, to discover whether they were common to expert witnesses in other medical specialties, and what was the perception of the legal profession of apparent conflict of opinion arising from different approaches in addressing these questions.

What has emerged is therefore to some extent an exploration of the philosophy of the basis of expert opinion. The concordance between the different specialties and between the medical and legal perceptions of the role of the expert witness is heartening: it may make it easier to address any difficulties encountered in practice in the adversarial system.

Other publications on expert evidence and the role of the expert witness are available, ranging from dissertations upon the law to practical guidance for the individual expert in a particular specialty. It is hoped that the converging viewpoints from different disciplines contained in this publication will be of interest to all those concerned with expert evidence, both giving and receiving, and may serve as a guide to those unsure as to 'how far they can go'.

STEPHEN LEADBEATTER

PART 1
THE LEGAL PERSPECTIVE

1 The criminal legal perspective

His Honour Judge Martin Stephens QC
Circuit Judge and Induction Course Director, Judicial Studies Board

The limitations of expert evidence in the criminal courts may be said to relate to two matters:

1. To the expert himself: is he one?

2. To the evidence he gives: to what extent can he be permitted to give an opinion based on his factual findings or on the findings of others?

This second aspect is of some considerable interest in the light of recent developments and will be discussed later.

Qualifications required by an expert witness

The question a judge must ask himself when presented with an alleged expert witness is whether he is qualified to give evidence on the relevant subject matter. For example, is the witness sufficiently competent or experienced to give expert evidence? What are his qualifications? How long has he worked in the field in which he is proposing to give evidence? Witnesses who present themselves to the courts as experts must be prepared to justify the appellation. Experienced expert witnesses know this, and will not only have set out their credentials in their proofs of evidence or reports but will willingly reel off the information when asked. Inexperienced witnesses will not; the sensible ones will be aware of their limitations and acknowledge them, whereas the less sensible will not do so and are likely to fail as witnesses.

Among the most vulnerable in the inexperienced category are young doctors from the casualty department who come to court to speak of wounds or bruising on a purely factual basis. It is notoriously difficult to be specific about bruising, in particular its age and causation. A young doctor who has not come to court as an expert witness but only as a witness of fact for the prosecution can find himself being questioned out of the blue about causation and age, sometimes by the prosecution, but more likely in cross-examination

by the defence. It is the judge's duty to step in when such questioning starts, to establish the status of the witness, and thus to determine whether he can give expert evidence.

However, I am afraid that some judges will not necessarily inter-
vene in this way. It is then up to the doctor to point out his lack
of experience or knowledge and to seek the judge's protection —
which should be given. The importance of this point was
emphasised in a recent Court of Appeal decision[1] which quashed a
conviction in a case in which an experienced medical orderly in the
Army had been permitted to give evidence of the cause of a wound
— whether it was a blunt instrument as opposed to a 'head-butt'.
The conviction was quashed because the orderly was not qualified to
give an opinion.

Knowledge based on a particular field of medicine together with
what I might call the 'consensus of informed opinion' on the subject in the acknowledged area of medical literature are the twin pre-
requisites for the expert witness. To this must be added as full as possible a knowledge of the facts of the case in which the expert
opinion is being sought. The expert will usually know that the other
side also has an expert witness and what he will say. Until comparatively recently this was not necessarily the case in criminal trials, but
rules introduced in 1987 now require advance disclosure to the
other side of all expert evidence that is to be relied upon. It is therefore particularly important that the expert witness should brief himself fully, not only on the acknowledged literature relating to the
matter in question but also on the evidence in the case. I recently
saw a rather cocksure counsel receive precisely what he deserved
when cross-examining an experienced consultant paediatrician in
relation to injuries to a child. He blithely asked a question, the gist
of which was: 'I suppose you have reminded yourself, doctor, of the
words of X and Y in this field as published in, let us say, the *Bavarian
Journal of Paediatrics* in 1992?'. 'Oh yes', replied the doctor, 'would
you like to see a copy? I have it here in my briefcase'. Collapse of
young cross-examining party.

The need for an expert witness to have all the qualities described
above is perhaps best illustrated by my experience at the Bar rather
than on the Bench where I now sit. When at the Bar, I was let down
more than once by experienced medical men, both outside court
and in the witness box. On one occasion the expert — having given
a bold and forthright opinion in writing and in conference, in the
full knowledge that the other side had an expert who disagreed fundamentally with his conclusions — backtracked to such an extent
outside the court door that we had to abandon that part of the case.

I seem to remember that the other side's man had been my man's professor at medical school, so I could only conclude that he had hoped that his mentor would not turn up in court on the day. On another occasion, I was even let down in evidence-in-chief (that is, when I was examining him myself) by my expert medical witness. He would not repeat in the witness box what he had told us in reports and in discussion beforehand.

Of course, no witness must give evidence inconsistent with his oath and if, as sometimes happens, he may be genuinely persuaded in cross-examination that his views are wrong, he must then say so. It is the preparation of his report and the thought, knowledge and research that go into it that are of critical importance.

Giving evidence in court

I do not intend to describe in detail how to give evidence in court but, knowing I was preparing this paper, a medical friend sent me a copy of a recent issue of the *British Medical Journal*,[2] in which there is a paragraph on how to be a better expert witness. I leave it to the reader to consider this worthy document at his leisure, but one or two gems are worth repeating here:

- Stand still, don't fidget.

- Avoid arguing with counsel; this will irritate the judge — [not with certain counsel it won't, the judge may well wish to get up and give you a big hug].

- Keep it simple, or the judge and jury may easily become lost — [too true].

The expert opinion

I turn now to the extent to which experts can be permitted to give an opinion in a criminal case. The classical exposition of the law in recent years on this matter was from Lord Justice Lawton in a case in 1974 called Turner,[3] from which I quote below.

An expert's opinion is admissible to furnish the court with scientific information which is likely to be outside the experience and knowledge of a judge or jury. If, on the proven facts, a judge or jury can form their own conclusions without help then opinion of an expert is unnecessary. In such a case, if given dressed up in scientific jargon, it may make judgment more difficult. The fact that an expert witness has impressive scientific qualification does

not by that fact alone make his opinion on matters of human
nature and behaviour within the limits of normality any more
helpful than that of the jurors themselves but there is a danger
that they may think it does.

I should like to stress the phrases 'if a judge or jury can form
their own conclusions without help', and 'behaviour within the
limits of normality'. In this particular case, a defendant on a charge
of murder was not permitted to call a psychiatrist to prove the
depth of his emotional state to support his defence of provocation,
which would of course have reduced the charge to manslaughter.
Lord Justice Lawton said that there was no authority in law for the
proposition that psychologists and psychiatrists can be called in all
cases to prove the probability of the accused's veracity; if any such
rule was applied to our courts, trial by psychiatrists would be likely
to take the place of trial by jury. He added: 'We do not find the
prospect attractive'.

The legal principles set out by the court in Turner's case still
hold sway. May I illustrate briefly by a case which I tried barely two
weeks ago. A young man of impeccable character was found late at
night sitting on a garden wall with a not very serious head injury.
Two experienced ambulance men did not think that he may have
been suffering from concussion and took him to a hospital for
'tidying up'. On the way to the hospital his behaviour started to
become bizarre and aggressive, culminating in quite a nasty attack
on nurses on arrival at the hospital.

The defence put forward in court was 'non-insane automatism'
(which, briefly, is involuntary movements of the body or limbs). A
consultant psychiatrist, who obviously had not examined the defendant at the time but had read all the documentation, was present in
court throughout the evidence. I allowed defence counsel to call
him and, after the preliminary matters, to ask him the following
question: 'Is all that you have heard in evidence and read in the
papers and the medical notes consistent with his acting in a state of
post-traumatic confusion?'. I did not allow the question which the
barrister first asked, which was: 'In your opinion, were his actions
carried out by reason of any confusional state?' — 'consistent with'
or 'were' being the distinction.

The reason for my refusal to allow the first question was because
whether he was acting in such a state was a matter for the jury and
not for the experts; in other words, it was the question of the 'ultimate issue', as it has been called, the very issue to be determined by
the jury. The old common law rule is just that: an expert witness

should not express an opinion on the ultimate issue — the issue which effectively has to be tried by a jury. However, in disallowing the one question and allowing the other, some would say that I may well have been acting in an overpunctilious and somewhat out-of-date manner.

In the circumstances of this particular case, I think my decision was right, but the rule itself is probably more honoured in the breach than in the observance. The Lord Chief Justice, Lord Taylor, as recently as 1993 said:

> The rationale behind the supposed prohibition is that the expert should not usurp the functions of the jury. But, since counsel can bring the witness so close to opining on the ultimate issue that the inference as to his view is obvious, the rule can only be a matter of form rather than substance. In our view, an expert is called to give his opinion and should be allowed to do so. It is, however, important that the judge should make clear to the jury that they are not bound by the expert's opinion.

So, when the expert now gives evidence he can expect to be asked his opinion, in certain cases, on the very issue to be tried by the jury and, unless he is stopped, he should boldly give it if he feels he can do so.

When an expert can and cannot give an opinion

Having said that, may I finally give three examples of the present state of the law where:

- an expert will be *required* to give an opinion;

- he will be *allowed* to give an opinion if he can; and,

- he will *not be allowed* to give an opinion.

These examples relate mainly to psychiatric evidence. As a circuit judge, not a high court judge, I see much less of pathologists now than when I was at the Bar. I then often heard the uniquely calm, almost self-effacing manner in which Professor Bernard Knight gave his evidence relating to all manner of dreadful deeds connected with violent death. A circuit judge is rarely allowed to try murders, although some of us are allowed to try rapes.

An expert is required to give an opinion

The first example is simple and straightforward. If there is a question of insanity or unfitness to plead, this issue can be decided only on the evidence of two or more medical practitioners who are approved under Section 12 of the Mental Health Act. This is where expert evidence is required before an issue can be decided.

An expert is allowed to give an opinion if he can

The second example comes from an area which doctors, in particular psychiatrists and psychologists, may find a growth area, that of the reliability of confessions. Recent notorious cases, as well as some less well publicised ones, have developed the law on this matter. In a case called Everett in 1988,[4] the judge ruled that evidence of admissions and confessions made to the police should not be excluded from the jury's consideration. The defendant was aged 42, but tests before his trial revealed a mental age of 8. He appealed against conviction on the ground that the evidence of his confession was wrongly admitted. The Court of Appeal, in quashing the conviction, held that the judge had been in error in deciding the question of admissibility simply by listening to the tapes of the interview carried out by the police officer and not taking into account medical evidence about the defendant's medical condition.

It is hard to believe that such a decision should have been made as recently as 1988. Lord Justice Watkins said:

> What the judge did was to rule in effect that he did not have to take account of the medical evidence of the mental condition of the appellant; on the contrary, he listened to the tape recording and expressed himself to be satisfied that the appellant had understood the questions and made rational answers to them. That is not the function of the judge in such a situation as this. He must regard the whole circumstances and take account of the medical evidence. Having done so, he may decide whether the prosecution has discharged the burden upon it and here it most certainly had not.

In a case called Raghip and others[5] (better known as the Winston Silcott case), where the prosecution had largely depended upon the defendant's confession, Lord Justice Farquharson said that the medical evidence before the Court of Appeal as to the defendant's mental capacity would have assisted the jury in assessing the mental condition of Mr Raghip and the consequent reliability of his alleged confession. The conviction was quashed after the Court of Appeal had listened to the evidence that the defendant was abnormally suggestible.

In Judith Ward's case, the admissibility of such evidence was confirmed to the fullest degree.[6] The Court of Appeal quashed her conviction after 20 years in jail for murder and causing explosions, thought to have been the work of the IRA. Much of the case there depended on her confessions. The Court of Appeal concluded that the expert evidence of a psychiatrist or a psychologist may properly be admitted if it is to the effect that the defendant is suffering from a condition not even properly described as mental illness, such as a personality disorder. In their view, such evidence is admissible on the issue of whether what a defendant has said in a confession or admission was reliable and, therefore, likely to have been true. The Court of Appeal went on to say that it thought the cases in which such evidence would properly be admissible would be comparatively rare.

An expert is not allowed to give an opinion

The third example is of a case where it is unlikely that expert evidence will be admissible. In 1993, the Court of Appeal made a decision[7] that what they called 'oath-helping' is not permitted: the prosecution cannot call a witness of fact and then call an expert medical witness to give evidence why that witness of fact is reliable. If the defence case is that the witness is unreliable because of some mental abnormality outside the jury's experience, it might be open to the prosecution to call evidence to rebut any such defence medical evidence but, in the usual case, such oath-helping evidence is not permitted.

Conclusion

I have touched on a few general and specific matters. The law is ever-changing and ever-developing, and the role of the expert witness is also developing and changing. If judges and juries will now have to grapple with the scientific, technical, statistical, actuarial and arithmetical arguments over DNA, I can see a time rapidly approaching when they will all have nervous breakdowns and expert witnesses will have to decide the cases for themselves.

References

1. *R v. Inch*, 91 Cr. App. R. 51.
2. Gulleford J. Preparing medical experts for the courtroom. *British Medical Journal* 1994;**309**:752–3.
3. *R v. Turner*, 60 Cr. App. R. 80.
4. *R v. Everett* [1988], Cr. L. R. 826.
5. *R v. Raghip and others* [1991], *The Times*, 9 December 1991.
6. *R v. Ward*, 96 Cr. App. R. 1.
7. *R v. Robinson*, 98 Cr. App. R. 370.

2 The civil perspective

Jennifer Cummin
Solicitor, Clyde & Co, London

It has been said that expert evidence is the Beecher's Brook of any civil action. It is the greatest hurdle you will encounter, and if you fail to clear it, you will not reach the finishing post.

It is difficult to identify the limitations on expert evidence because they are interwoven throughout the whole of civil proceedings. The term 'medico-legal' is a very user friendly term and it pops up all over the place. We have 'medico-legal advisers', 'medico-legal representatives', but what does the term actually mean? In my view a more accurate description would be 'medico-legal divide', because when it comes to civil proceedings, 'medical' and 'legal' are very distinct entities.

Medical experts date back many years. In Europe, they were used for religious reasons; the Roman Catholic Church used experts to illustrate false miracles and other interesting phenomena, for example bees don't sting virgins! In England, in 1345, surgeons were first called to court to show that a wound was fresh. We have come a long way since then, but there is one paramount feature, which is that an expert has a duty to the court.

How do civil and criminal proceedings differ? The bottom line is that civil proceedings are about money, about financial compensation for a plaintiff who alleges that the defendant's negligence has caused him an injury. There are two types of financial compensation; the first is what lawyers call 'pain, suffering and loss of amenity' and refers to the injury suffered by the plaintiff and the way in which it has adversely affected his life. The second is financial loss, namely financial loss from the past, present and future.

In order to succeed, the plaintiff must prove three separate heads; firstly, that the medical practitioner owed him a duty of care. Secondly, that there was a breach of that duty, ie the defendant was negligent and the plaintiff suffered an injury. Thirdly, the plaintiff must prove 'causation', ie the negligence actually caused the injury to the plaintiff.

To give an example, during the course of an uneventful operation, a grey mass near the femoral nerve, unassociated with the operation, was excised. The next day the patient got up and fell over, because he had lost the use of his leg. This was due to the femoral nerve having been severed. Was there negligence and causation? You have to examine the three heads; first, was there a duty of care? The answer is yes. The medical practitioner had a duty of care to the patient. Secondly, was there a breach? Clearly there was because expert opinion was of the view that one would not excise a mass so close to the femoral nerve but would take a biopsy first, especially as it was unrelated to the operation and it was not a life-threatening situation. Thirdly, was it causative? Undoubtedly it was because the severance of the femoral nerve caused the loss of the use of the leg.

To what extent does the plaintiff have to prove the three heads? He has to prove them on the balance of probabilities, ie, it is more likely than not that the negligence caused the injury.

These different heads require separate expert reports. The first would be to consider the skill of the medical practitioner involved, ie, the negligence. The second would consider the physical evidence, ie, causation.

The expert within the framework of a civil action

How does the expert get his evidence across to the court and to his legal representatives? There are two ways: by written report and later, from oral evidence in court. I shall now look at the nuts and bolts of a civil action to illustrate how expert evidence, both written and oral, is interwoven throughout this procedure. I will refer to what I call 'the ten steps' from the beginning to the end of a civil action.

Step one is 'the letter before action'. This is the letter sent by the plaintiff's solicitors to the defendant, stating on the information held they have a meritorious case and requesting disclosure of all the relevant records and documentation. This normally has to be given. Upon receipt of the documents, the plaintiff's expert is kicked into play, and considers whether they support the plaintiff's case. This is a very important step; most plaintiffs in negligence cases are on legal aid, and the legal aid certificate will not be extended if the expert is of the view at this early stage that there is no case. If the plaintiff is privately funded, he would be a fool to consider taking on such a financial burden without the support of expert opinion.

If there is a case, step two is the plaintiff's issue of proceedings and service of the Statement of Claim. The latter is a legal document setting out the plaintiff's case — the issues, the allegations of negligence, the injuries and the loss suffered. The drafting of this document requires the cooperation of the expert, in order to guide the lawyers in the understanding and drafting of the medical and forensic issues.

The defence now springs into action, and step three is the service of the defendant's Defence. The expert for the defence will guide the lawyers as to the response to the issues in the Statement of Claim and which matters to raise in the defence.

Step four is when the opposing party can request further details about the Statement of Claim or the defence, by way of a legal document called 'the further and better particulars'. The experts will advise on which additional details to request, and consider any details so received.

Step five comprises the instructions to the expert to draft the expert report. This will be a formal letter of instruction from solicitors which will set out all the facts in the case, all the documentation and what issues the parties are trying to prove or refute. These are the expert's terms of reference from which the expert report will be drafted. The drafting of the expert report comprises step six and further details about that report are discussed below.

Step seven consists of the exchange of expert reports by all parties. This is to stop 'trial by ambush'; both parties are entitled to see the 'substance' of the other party's expert evidence. What does 'substance' mean? In practice, the whole expert report is usually exchanged.

Step eight involves the meeting of the experts from both parties. This can be by agreement or by order of the court, to allow the experts to ascertain the areas of agreement and disagreement. This is a growing trend and is becoming more common in litigation. There are merits and dangers with such meetings. Usually the experts agree on most of the reports, and isolate a few areas where interpretations differ. This can help to clarify the real issues upon which to concentrate. The dangers are that additional issues come to light or that one party reveals areas damaging to their case.

Step nine involves either proceeding to trial as to whether the defendant is liable, or the defendant admitting liability and negotiating a settlement. Trial or settlement very much depends on the strength of each party's expert evidence, and the legal advisers will be guided by the expert opinion on the strengths and weaknesses of the case.

Step ten involves quantum, ie, the amount of damages due to the plaintiff. If a case is settled, quantum will be agreed. If there is disagreement, quantum will be decided by the judge at trial. Only about 2% of cases proceed to trial. The chances are the expert will not have to attend trial, but it is never safe to rely on that. The expert must assume the case will go all the way to trial, from the first letter of instruction, and he must be prepared to go all the way with it.

The format of the expert report

When the written expert report is considered in more detail, the 'medico-legal divide' can be seen very clearly. With regard to that report, the expert may say 'this is my document; you have asked me to advise and I have advised'. But it must also be remembered that the report is a legal document and there are certain criteria and formats to which it must adhere. So let us consider how an aspiring expert may be advised on the preparation of a report.

You will receive a letter of instruction, from solicitors, which provides your terms of reference. The solicitor will send you the tools of your trade, which are the records, the charts, the X-rays — anything you need to consider before giving an opinion. Do not be shy about asking for any additional material. Do not assume that the solicitor has understood it all and sent you everything you need. You are the expert, the solicitor is not. For example, you might find there are documents or records referred to which you have not received or only you may realise the significance of having sight of the original documents rather than copies.

What about the format of the expert report itself? Unfortunately, there is no official format. So what should you include in your expert report? I have produced the following check list:

■ You should include an introduction about yourself — your expertise, your qualifications, the positions you have held, any publications you have written, lectures you have given, committees you have sat on, etc.

■ You should include details about the nature of the dispute you have been asked to comment on. It is worthwhile having a paragraph about what the dispute actually concerns, so that there is no disagreement about how *you* see it and how you have been *told* it is.

■ You should then include a paragraph concerning your specific instructions. Those instructions will be contained in the letter of instruction from the solicitor. It is worthwhile stating who instructed you, who you are acting for and what precisely you have been asked to do.

- Include a paragraph about documentation: set out what documents you have been given and what you have had sight of.

- Give details about the dispute itself: you want to distinguish between the facts that you have been given, the facts that you have been told are in dispute, and the facts that you have been asked to assume.

- Give details about the issues themselves: each party's views, your instructions on those views and what you are going to address.

- Give details about your first practical involvement in the case; you are likely to carry out some form of examination or some investigation. If you have examined the plaintiff, give details of that examination. If you have carried out an experiment, give details of all the data and what you were seeking to ascertain.

All the matters I have referred to so far have been of a factual nature. You should now proceed to stating your own opinion.

- Distinguish what facts your opinion is based on — the facts that you have been given, the facts that you have been asked to assume and the facts that you found out yourself from your own investigations or examinations. Also include opinions from other texts or publications which you might wish to rely on. You are entitled to refer to such publications, as long as you state that that is what you are doing and give specific references.

- Then you come to the conclusion: this will pull everything together — your opinions and your reasons for reaching them on each issue.

- Finally sign and date the report.

- You might wish to have an appendix or a number of appendices, to include additional details rather than including them in the body of the report. For example, you might want an appendix containing more specific details of the experiments or investigations you may have carried out. You will certainly

want one referring to any text and publications that you have
adopted and opinions to which you have referred.

Once you have submitted your report to the lawyers, they may ask
you to consider certain amendments. Remember your report will be
disclosed to the opposing party.

In this regard there must be mutual respect between the lawyer
and the expert. If you are asked to amend the report, it is usually for
some tactical reason — reference to a privileged document, or a
different format is preferred. The best guideline I can give is that
the report should not be changed to such an extent that you can no
longer agree with its *content*. You have a duty to the court, and your
report must be an independent product based on your own
opinions. You are not merely a mouthpiece for the client. Also,
whatever the legal proceedings demand of you, you must not
change your opinion or your views. If you are pushed into a corner
where you are being asked to adopt an approach you do not agree
with, then you must say 'If this is what you want of me, I cannot give
it'. It is better to say so at this early stage rather than wait until you
are in the court room.

There must be no legal submissions in the report either. There
must be no judgments. It is a matter for the judge to decide whether
there was negligence and causation. This is a very fine line, because
it may be difficult for you not to reach those conclusions. However
it will be clear from your opinion whether or not you consider there
was any negligence. So leave the ultimate issue to the judge; do not
take on that burden.

The expert in court

One hopes that when the report is disclosed, the opposing party will
immediately back off with tail between legs. Unfortunately, this
rarely happens. Once the reports are disclosed, more issues come to
the fore. If called to give evidence in court, assume the case is going
to trial. It might settle on the steps, but do not assume it will.

The court is a very lonely place for an expert. You are the
messenger of the expert evidence, and as much as your evidence will
be assessed by the judge, so are you. Your evidence can be limited by
the way in which you present it — it is not enough for the words to
speak for themselves; the way that you present them will also carry
weight.

There was a very famous forensic expert called Sir Bernard
Spilsbury, who died in 1947, who was described as follows:

Juries are formed from men and women of the public and the public believed Spilsbury was infallible. Spilsbury had indeed done what few can hope to do. He had become a legend in his own lifetime. His pronouncements were invested with the force of dogma and it was blasphemy to hint that he might conceivably be wrong.[1]

If Spilsbury was on your case, you were home and dry, but I am afraid this does not happen to most of us. So, what are your limitations in court? Everything you intended to say should have been included in your expert report. It is fair to say that new issues come up in court all the time, but if there were issues which you could have included and you had all the evidence to do so but did not, and you raise these issues for the first time in court, all hell will break loose. The opposing party will be taken by surprise; they will say 'You cannot adduce that evidence'. At best, they might ask for an adjournment and be granted it. There will be cost implications for that and everyone will be glaring at you. So check with the solicitor that everything required is in the report, to cover yourself.

Do not answer anything that is not within your speciality; you might find that counsel will push you to give your opinion — firmly decline to answer.

Be prepared to concede something if it is appropriate to do so. If you have made an error, concede it. If a good point has been put to you, with which you agree, concede it. There are no merits in being dogmatic for the sake of it.

They say that 'lawyers earn a living by the sweat of their brow-beating' and that is true in cross-examination. Cross-examining counsel will try and undermine you; he will try and make you change your opinion. If he is unable to do so he will at best try to show that you are not as credible as his own expert.

Cross-examination is a difficult task for the expert to deal with; being asked questions by a non-expert, albeit a specialist lawyer, can be irritating and frustrating. You must have sympathy with the lawyers — and the judge — as they are unlikely to understand the subject like you, the expert. You must get your expertise across to them. If they are getting shirty about it, that is a fault on their part. This is the best way to think it through, to prevent yourself becoming angry or ruffled.

Again, be kind to the judge. He is in a very difficult position. If he chooses one expert against another, he is effectively saying to one expert 'I don't find you credible'; or 'I don't hold with any of your opinions'. Judges do not like doing that — and neither would you if you were in their position. So, show them 'the way home'; show them the various interpretations and why you adhere to your own. Allow the judge leeway to choose between differing interpretations.

After the court case you may have won or lost. If you have lost, do not let this colour your views or your views of yourself as an expert. Talk to your counsel afterwards and find out what went wrong and what went right — nobody wins 100% of the time, and the experience of any case can assist the next.

I will conclude by taking a global view of experts. There has always been controversy about expert evidence, which can be illustrated in such cases as the 'Dingo baby', the 'Guildford four', the 'Birmingham six'. Now that is not to say there should never be critical examination of a system, but at the same time, it should be recognised for what it is. In my view, you cannot better an expert in his speciality, giving oral evidence in court, giving his honest opinion and being tried and tested under cross-examination.

I have referred to the 'medico-legal divide'. It affects the expert and the presentation of expert evidence. But one thing is worth remembering; if a case is about to come to trial and the allocated judge cannot sit, another judge can be allocated. If counsel is engaged on another case, another counsel can be instructed. But if the expert is unavailable, the case grinds to a halt. It cannot proceed. The expert with his expert evidence is fundamental and that must be the greatest 'medico-legal divide' of all.

Reference

1.   From *Anonymous letters to the Press,* cited in Burns C R, ed, *Legacies in Law & Medicine.* Canton: Watson Pub Intl, 1977.

PART 2

THE MEDICAL AND SCIENTIFIC PERSPECTIVE

3 Clinical evidence

Roger C Evans
Consultant in Emergency Medicine, The Accident Unit, Cardiff Royal Infirmary

The chance of a doctor being caught up in the medico-legal process has increased significantly over recent years for several reasons, one of which is the greater frequency with which patients are prepared to turn to the law in order to right a perceived wrong. Doctors may be asked to provide expert opinions in cases of alleged medical negligence, either for the plaintiff or for the defendant. Doctors also have to give statements of fact to the police in a wide variety of cases, including sensitive areas such as matrimonial disputes or child sex abuse. Any of these statements or reports may lead to an appearance in court as a witness of fact or opinion. Doctors working in certain fields such as obstetrics, orthopaedics and emergency medicine are perhaps more likely to be involved than others, but no discipline is exempt — even those which are laboratory based.

Some idea of the spread of litigation can be obtained from an article by Gwynne[1] in the *Proceedings of the Royal College of Physicians of Edinburgh*, in which he analysed 500 consecutive claims of medical negligence over about three years (Table 1).

Why do patients resort to legal proceedings?

The obvious answer to the question why patients resort to legal proceedings would be because there has been an actual or perceived mistake in medical or nursing management which the plaintiff feels has caused him unnecessary pain and suffering (either physical or mental), and may also have placed him at a financial disadvantage. However, in a review of some 350 cases of actions against accident and emergency (A&E) departments in various parts of the UK, I found certain other complaints cropped up consistently and seem to have played their part in stimulating the plaintiff to lodge a claim.

Rude and uncaring treatment

It was common to find remarks to the effect that the medical or nursing staff had been perceived by the patient and/or his relatives to be, at best, totally uninterested in or, at worst, downright rude to, the plaintiff. The words 'abrupt', 'condescending' and 'judgmental' were often used, and in many cases the feelings engendered by these perceptions were aggravated by a prolonged wait to be seen and treated.

Unrealistic expectations

Patients' expectations of what modern medicine can achieve with regard both to morbidity and to mortality were often unrealistic. There was frequently the impression that the plaintiff and/or his relatives felt that nobody should die or be left with a significant disability following an accident or acute illness and, if this did happen, it was someone's fault.

This attitude was sometimes reinforced by members of the medical profession. Throwaway lines such as 'He'll be as good as new, my dear' were taken literally, and when the desired result was not forthcoming, the comment was handed on verbatim to a lawyer.

Table 1
500 consecutive medical negligence claims between 1 April 1990 and 31 July 1993 broken down by specialty.[1]

Specialty	No.	%
Obstetrics (70) & gynaecology (67)	137	27
Surgery	82	16
Orthopaedics	65	13
Medicine	44	8
Accident & emergency	39	8
Anaesthetics	27	5
Paediatrics	25	5
Neurosurgery	21	4
Psychiatry	15	3
Ophthalmology	13	3
Dental	12	2
Radiology	9	2
Ear, nose & throat	7	1
Others	4	1
Total	*500*	

It is much more appropriate to give a realistic and, where necessary, guarded prognosis, rather than to make an ill-judged attempt to cheer up the patient and his relatives.

Inadequate analgesia

I am often impressed by the stoicism exhibited by many of my colleagues in the face of their patients' pain.

A recurring complaint in patients' statements was that they felt the level of pain they had been allowed to suffer was unappreciated, and that no effective analgesia was offered over a prolonged period. Whilst it is inappropriate to dispense strong controlled drugs thoughtlessly, withholding pain relief is totally unjustifiable.

'Advised to sue'

In over 30% of the cases reviewed, the patients felt that they had been advised or encouraged to resort to the legal process by a member of one of the caring professions. It seems that a large percentage of doctors cannot resist making derogatory remarks about a patient's management by doctors from a different hospital or even by those working in another department of the same institution. A wide variety of members of the caring professions seem prepared to suggest to patients that their previous management has been less than adequate.

There is no doubt that the 'encouragement' the patient feels he has received is often no more than an aside to a colleague. However, more often than I would have thought possible, someone has written an inappropriate comment in the patient's notes. Whilst I would not suggest that unsatisfactory practices be covered up, many of these comments were by people working outside the discipline involved and whose depth of knowledge in that field was very much open to question.

Fact or opinion?

It is important that a doctor involved in medico-legal matters distinguishes between a statement of *fact* and one of *opinion*. When asked for a statement of fact, the doctor should stick rigidly to the details recorded in the patient's notes and resist attempts to be drawn into speculation, for instance, how the patient acquired the injury. It may be appropriate to go as far as to say that the injury was 'consistent with' one of a variety of mechanisms, but unless you actually witnessed the event much of what you say will be based on hearsay evidence — that is, what the patient told you in his history.

Liability and causation

If the doctor is instructed to produce a medical report on the basis of his expertise in a discipline, he may be asked to comment on two aspects:

- *Liability* in simple terms means 'Was a mistake made?'. For instance, 'Was there a failure to identify obvious acute ischaemic changes on an ECG, and was the patient discharged instead of being admitted?'.

- *Causation* deals with the consequences of that mistake: 'Did the patient die or fail to receive timely thrombolytic treatment because of that error, and therefore suffered as a result?'.

The opinion

The medical expert witness should provide a balanced independent opinion in terms that are comprehensible to the plaintiff and his legal advisers. Where, as commonly happens, conflicting accounts are received from the plaintiff and the defendant, it is not the expert's place to decide whose account is the accurate one — this must be left to the judge.

If writing a report on behalf of the plaintiff, you may need to accept the patient's account and offer an opinion on that basis, but also to devote a section of the report to what the defence will say based on the hospital's account and on the contemporaneous notes.

The perceived error may have been made by a junior member of staff, so the expert must put himself in the position of that doctor and realistically assess what someone with that level of expertise could reasonably be expected to achieve. The same standards cannot be expected from a senior house officer (SHO) working in an A&E department as from a consultant cardiologist in his outpatient clinic.

Matters to be considered in forming an opinion

No doctor is expected to get the diagnosis right every time, but is expected to work to a satisfactory standard and to use currently accepted diagnostic and therapeutic methods. To win a case, it is necessary to prove that the patient's management fell below the standard of a reasonably competent practitioner in that discipline. In general, the most effective criticisms of management are those that can be backed up by references to authoritative texts in the relevant field, particularly British ones. It is considered that a defence against such allegation would be to prove that a substantial body of reputable medical opinion working in that specialty would have managed the case in the same way, even if, in retrospect, they were found to have been mistaken.

It is important to remember that in civil proceedings of this nature you are working not on a basis of 'beyond a reasonable doubt' but on 'the balance of probabilities'. In percentage terms, this means that, instead of being 99% certain as in the criminal case, there only has to be a 51%/49% balance in the plaintiff's favour.

Lord Scarman, in the case of Maynard[2] versus the West Midlands Regional Health Authority, pointed out that:

> A case which is based on an allegation that a fully considered decision of consultants in the field of their special skill was negligent, clearly presents certain difficulties of proof. It is not enough to show that there is a body of competent professional opinion which considers that it was the wrong decision, if there is a body of professional opinion equally competent, which supports the decision as reasonable in the circumstances.

It is also important that the patient has been satisfactorily advised/warned of the risks of the treatment he is about to undergo, particularly where surgery is contemplated or an investigation is significantly invasive.

A further judgment by Lord Scarman in the case of Sidaway versus Bethlem Royal Hospital and the Maudsley Hospital Health Authority,[3] states that:

> I think that English law must recognise a duty on the doctor to warn his patient of risk inherent in the treatment which he is proposing; and especially so if the treatment be surgery. The critical limitation is that the duty is confined to material risk. The test of materiality is whether in the circumstances of the particular case the court is satisfied that a reasonable person in the patient's position would be likely to attach significance to the risk. Even if the risk be material, the doctor will not be liable, if upon a reasonable assessment of his patient's condition he takes the view that such a warning would be detrimental to his patient's health.

Whilst the health authority/hospital trust is considered to be responsible for the actions of the doctor/nurse whom it has employed, it must also ensure that this professional is adequately trained and supported to undertake the tasks expected of him.

Lord Justice Mustill, in the case of Wilsher versus Essex Area Health Authority,[4] put it thus:

> If a doctor is put into a position in which he or she is insufficiently experienced to meet the demands of the job, then whilst the doctor's degree of competence may be sufficient to enable him or her personally to defend a claim of negligence, a patient may seek redress against that doctor's employer (ie the health authority) alleging negligence in allocating an inexperienced doctor to a post in which a patient is entitled to expect greater competence in treatment.

Advocacy

The British legal system is adversarial, which can predispose some expert witnesses who have a competitive personality to overstate their case. It is important to offer whoever seeks advice the best possible opinion, but it must be both realistic and objective. The plaintiff will have an advocate in the barrister representing him: it is the job of the expert witness to provide the lawyer with accurate information, not to be an advocate himself.

It should also be remembered that only rarely is the situation 'black and white', and counsel should also be made aware, as far as possible, of what the other side may allege.

The report

It is vital that the report is based on all the relevant documentation — which of course includes radiographs, cardiograms, etc. If a report is based on only part of the available documentation, there is a risk of initiating or prolonging an expensive and (for the defendant) unpleasant experience.

Quality of documentation

One of the major limitations in the preparation of a report is the quality of the notes received. To a certain extent, this also means the quality of the photocopies, but it is mainly the calibre of the doctors' and nurses' entries in the patient's notes. In my experience, the quality of note taking across the whole breadth of medicine is poor, making it almost impossible to defend some cases.

Language of the report

I would recommend the use of precise and temperate language in the report or statement — and extend this advice to comments made in patients' notes as everything written there is now discoverable. Intemperate language is also dangerous in that it can inflame an already fraught situation and give the plaintiff or his relatives unrealistic expectations.

It is relevant to point out that there have been several cases in recent years in which doctors have faced not civil but criminal charges as a result of their alleged negligence. The use of terms such as 'criminally negligent' is therefore to be discouraged. A doctor may feel it reasonable to appear in court where the sanction is purely financial, but hesitate to undertake this task in a case in which, for instance, an SHO in oncology is facing a manslaughter charge. Many people who take legal action are upset — often understandably — perhaps by the death of a loved one, and actually want revenge, not financial compensation.

The legal profession has an important duty to inform clients as to the results of the judicial process in this type of case. They should ensure that the plaintiff is aware that in the vast majority of cases a successful action will confirm their assertion that the treatment was below a standard which could reasonably have been expected and they will then be financially compensated for this. It is not the job of the law to humiliate and verbally flog the doctor who, the plaintiff feels, has erred.

Where does your expertise lie?

It is not uncommon to be asked to give an expert opinion in a case which touches only marginally on your area of expertise. Solicitors who practise solely in the negligence field become very knowledgeable and rarely make this type of mistake. However, some solicitors who are not specialised in the medical negligence field are unaware that a doctor who in the past has given an opinion in a personal injury case is not equally qualified to comment on the appropriateness or otherwise of, say, a cardiologist's management of ischaemic heart disease.

It is foolish to accept such briefs. Given the scope of modern medicine, it is impossible to maintain the appropriate standard of expertise in areas outside your own. A carefully researched report might slip through the initial stages of the process, but rest assured that when you are in the witness box and the opposition's barrister (with a cardiologist sitting next to him) starts to question you, you will realise that you are about to go through an experience which will not be life-enhancing!

Conclusion

I think it is important that the expert witness should always try to understand the situation faced by the defendant at the time of the alleged incident, and appreciate — if not necessarily excuse — why the situation worked out the way it did. Few people never make mistakes, which is important to remember when formulating a report.

References

1. Gwynne AL. Patients, doctors and lawyers. *Proceedings of the Royal College of Physicians of Edinburgh* 1994;**24**:60–4.

2. *Maynard v. West Midlands Regional Health Authority* [1984] 1WLR 635 HL.

3. *Sidaway v. Board of Governors of the Bethlem Royal Hospital and the Maudsley Hospital* [1985] 2WLR 480 HL.

4. *Wilsher v. Essex Area Health Authority* [1988] 2WLR 557 HL.

4 DNA: Scientific and legal issues

Part 1 — Scientific issues

Patrick J Lincoln
Reader in Haemogenetics, The London Hospital Medical College

The instructions which determine whether a person has blood group A, B, AB or O, as well as the information for every other physical characteristic, are carried by the genetic material, deoxyribonucleic acid (DNA). Almost every cell in the human body carries the same set of DNA, half of which is inherited from each parent. This DNA is found within the nucleus of the cell on structures called chromosomes and is composed of two complementary thread-like strands of chemical building blocks.

It has been recognised for some time that if the actual genetic material could be studied, rather than the products whose synthesis it controls, we would have a tool, first, that could identify enormous variation and, secondly, if sufficient DNA could be examined, in theory people could be identified uniquely because the total DNA of no two individuals except identical twins will be the same. Investigation of the actual structure of the DNA has so much more potential as far as the identification of individuals is concerned. This is because most of the DNA which shows such enormous inter-individual variation does not, as far as we know, control the synthesis of end products such as blood groups or physical characteristics which can be detected. The tests that forensic scientists can use at the present time investigate only a fraction of the total DNA, and so cannot identify individuals uniquely, but the level of individualisation that can be attained has increased dramatically with the application of the current DNA technology. This brings a significant step closer the ultimate goal of unique genetic identification.

Variation in the DNA

The type of variation occurring in the DNA that is of interest to forensic scientists for identification purposes exists because small sections of DNA building blocks are repeated next to each other. The repeated sections can be present in different numbers, so the

particular region where these occur can vary in length in different
individuals. This means that when such a region of the thread of
DNA is cut out, using chemical scissors called restriction enzymes
(which cut the thread at specific points), the lengths of the result-
ing fragments vary according to the number of building blocks they
contain. An individual will carry two versions of each such region of
DNA; these can vary in length, one having been inherited from each
parent.

Detection of the variation

The DNA testing that has been mostly used by forensic scientists up
to now involves, first, the extraction and purification of the DNA
from the sample material (eg liquid blood, saliva, semen stain,
blood stain). The long thread-like structures of DNA are subse-
quently cut into fragments using restriction enzymes. It is these
fragments that can vary in length depending on how many of the
short specific sequences of DNA lie between the points at which the
thread of DNA is cut.

The fragments are sorted according to their size by electro-
phoresis in which they are subjected to an electric current whilst
being held in a jelly-like medium (gel). The sample DNA is loaded
into wells at one end, and over a period of time the fragments move
through the gel driven by the electric current. The smallest fragments, less constrained by the gel, move fastest and further from the
origin than the larger fragments which will move more slowly.

The fragments are then fixed into the position to which they
have moved by blotting on to a nylon membrane. The position to
which each fragment has moved can be visualised by the use of a
'probe', a synthetically produced piece of DNA whose chemical
structure is homologous to the repeated chemical sequence in the
fragments to be identified. The probe is labelled with a radioactive
or chemical marker. Because of their related structures, the probe
binds to the fragments of interest. The position of the probe, and
hence of the fragment, can then be identified. The labelled probes
will blacken a photographic plate; black bands are seen on the
plate, each corresponding to fragments of a particular length.
Increasingly, non-radioactive means of detection are used, whereby
the chemical label on the probe initiates a chemical reaction producing light which blackens the photographic film.

Single locus probe tests

The most widely used technique up to the present time has been single locus probe testing by which the different sizes of fragments that can occur at a single point or locus along the thread of DNA are investigated. By selecting probes with different chemical structures, it is possible to look at different regions or loci along the threads of DNA (cf different blood group systems). A series of probes is generally used, each identifying fragments from a different region/locus that shows variation, to build up a DNA profile of the individual. This can be achieved by retesting with the different probes the nylon membrane that carries the fragments produced by the cutting of the threads and subsequent sorting using an electric current.

Each individual has a genetic contribution from each parent, so two fragments will be present in each test and two bands are normally seen. Since so many different sizes of fragments can occur at each location along the DNA threads, only rarely will the same size of fragment be inherited from both parents. If it is, only one band is then seen in the individual, corresponding to the two fragments of the same size.

Matching DNA profiles

The aim of the DNA profiling test in forensic problems is usually to determine whether material (blood stain, semen, or some other body fluid or tissue) found at the scene of crime could have been left by the suspect. Since all the cells of the body carry the same DNA, the same fragments will be present, irrespective of whether they originate from DNA from hair, blood or semen, and comparison of DNA profiles can be made using, say, blood from the suspect and semen from the scene of crime.

The black bands produced on the photographic films can be compared to see if they match in position. The position of the band on the film corresponds to the size of the fragment producing it, so visual comparison of the position of bands provides an assessment of whether fragments from different samples are from the same source. Such a first visual comparison can be most satisfactorily made when the relevant samples have been tested at the same time and are on the same photographic film.

The sizes of the fragments producing the bands in the test samples can be estimated by including in each test run standard markers (ladders) composed of many fragments of known size. These can be used as a gauge: by comparing the positions of the bands in the test material with the positions of the bands produced by the fragments of known sizes in the ladder, an estimate of the sizes of the fragments in the test material can be made. Comparing these estimated fragment sizes is another way of assessing whether or not fragments from two samples match.

Such fragment sizes can be used to make a comparison when samples are run at the same time or when they are tested on different occasions; in addition, the estimated sizes can be recorded and stored for future reference. Clearly, if fragments from two samples do not match, either visually or by size, this can provide evidence of non-identity (ie exclusion of a person as the donor of a stain).

Assessment of significance of matching profiles

If the DNA bands/fragments detected in the suspect and the crime scene sample are considered to match, the significance of this finding is determined by a knowledge of the frequency of occurrence of individuals with bands which would be considered to match. The relevant question is what is the probability that the suspect will have matching bands by chance if he is innocent and did not leave this semen/blood stain at the scene of crime? To answer this, the frequency of occurrence in the population of all the various sized fragments from the different regions of the DNA tested must be known. Such frequencies are obtained by testing large numbers of individuals to build up a database of information, so that reliable estimates can be made of the frequency with which a particular fragment occurs.

The frequency with which the individual bands are found to occur in the population may not be particularly uncommon, for instance, 10%. However, if the results of three or four single locus tests identifying two fragments from each location are considered, the chance of an individual having matching bands through chance rather than because the stain came from his body fluid may be as low as one in millions. Since genetic material is passed from parents to children, the chances of finding the same bands in closely related individuals such as brothers will be vastly greater. The frequency with which some fragments are found to occur can also vary according to the ethnic origin of the individual, so databases have had to be constructed from the results of tests performed on individuals from different racial groups. In the UK, these usually consist of Caucasian, Asian and Afro-Caribbean individuals.

Variation in fragment size

The process of matching DNA profiles and the subsequent assessment of their frequency of occurrence may appear straightforward, but these procedures are not without their problems. One problem is that there can be slight variation in the position to which a fragment moves under the influence of the electric current. Thus, the same sample or different samples from the same source (eg semen stain and blood sample from the same man) may not move to exactly matching positions when tested on different occasions — or even when tested together on the same occasion.

How much allowance to make for this variation has to be determined by experiment by each laboratory. When the extent of the variation that can occur in the laboratory is known, allowance can be made for it when deciding whether or not two bands match either by visual comparison or by fragment size. Fragment size will also show variation since it is determined by the positions of the bands on the film. In addition, this variation becomes relevant when the database is used to determine the frequency of a particular fragment among individuals. The information in the database is obtained from testing many individuals. This will, of necessity, be performed over a period of time, so that fragments of the same size may have been assigned slightly different values on different occasions.

If the allowance that needs to be made for the variation is underestimated, fewer individuals will be included in the category of those having bands/fragments which must be considered to match and, therefore, there will be an underestimate of their frequency.

Validity of fragment frequency data

In cases where there is a match, for instance, when the suspect is not excluded as the donor of a stain, the final conclusion of the forensic scientist will be in the form of a frequency with which such DNA fragments would be expected to be found in the relevant population — for example, one in a million unrelated white British individuals may be expected to have fragments which would have to be considered to match those found in the stain. The accuracy of these figures, the question of what is the relevant population, whether the sample of individuals tested for the database is representative and sufficient in number, and whether the test systems are genetically independent of each other and can be combined, have all been the subject of considerable debate. The interpretation of the significance of the results in terms of guilt or innocence has also been called into question, especially in the criminal courts by defence lawyers seeking to test the validity of what appears to be overwhelming prosecution evidence.

Polymerase chain reaction — an alternative method of DNA testing

DNA technology is changing all the time. More recent developments enable the forensic scientist to utilise polymerase chain reaction (PCR) technology to obtain useful information from minute amounts of material, even when degraded, that have previously been untestable. With PCR, it is possible to copy small sections of the DNA in a test-tube, which can result in a many million-fold increase in the amount of DNA available for testing. For forensic applications, the sections of DNA copied/multiplied in this way are regions which show interindividual variability, in some instances in the same way as the fragments described above in single locus probe testing.

The main advantage of such PCR-based testing is that it can be carried out on very small samples which would normally yield insufficient DNA for successful testing. In addition, it can be used where the DNA is broken down or degraded, such as when the stain material is old or has been subjected to unfavourable conditions such as washing.

As well as increasing the amount of DNA, the PCR methodology also selects out for multiplication the specific section of DNA which it is proposed to investigate. The products can then be examined to see if they match or are the same type when they are compared from the various samples under investigation.

A series of test systems that has recently joined the repertoire of forensic scientists — because they can be detected using such PCR technology — are the short tandem repeat (STR) systems. As with DNA single locus probe test systems, the interindividual variation in the length of DNA fragments is examined, but with STR systems the repeated sections of DNA, and consequently the fragments, are much shorter. A major difference to the previously used systems, based on differences in fragment length, is that there are far fewer possible lengths of fragments in each test system, typically perhaps only 6–12 compared to more than 100. This means that each test system has a lower discriminating power than DNA single locus probe systems, so a larger number of such STR test systems are needed to achieve similar levels of discrimination.

However, another effect of this reduced number of fragments is that they can be sized with considerably greater accuracy. More precise categorisation can be made of the fragments, so the results can be given as types, rather like conventional blood grouping types. Ultimately, the type of fragment detected is identified by the number of short sections of DNA that compose the fragment and give it its specific length, so that the type is given simply as a number. As in other DNA test systems, two fragments are present in each individual, one having been inherited from each parent. A different size of fragment is sometimes inherited from each parent, but it is not unusual for an individual to inherit the same size of fragment from each parent because of the smaller number of alternative sizes of fragments that occur.

A further advantage of these STR typing systems is that they are more amenable to automation. Separation under the influence of the electric current of the fragments produced by the multiplication in the PCR technique, the subsequent identification of their position in the gel and hence their size, can all be automated and computer-controlled.

Comparison of the results obtained is simply a matter of whether or not the same types, shown as numbers, exist in the two samples being compared. Non-matching samples showing different types cannot originate from the same individual. When they match, a statistical assessment has to be made of the significance of this finding. Databases have to be compiled of information concerning the frequency with which the different types occur in individuals in the various ethnic groups. Their use to assess the frequency of occurrence is more straightforward than for single locus testing; fragment types are specifically determined, and the allowances that have to be made for variation in determining single locus fragment sizes are not necessary. Evidence towards positive identity still rests on a calculation of probability.

Conclusions

There seems little doubt that the introduction of DNA technology to problems of identification in the forensic context has been the most dramatic development in forensic science. It offers the potential of very powerful evidence, either in terms of non-identity or towards positive identity. This applies especially to the field of sexual assaults, where body fluids under investigation are other than blood, and the number of conventional markers detectable will be few and have limited potential in terms of discriminating power.

DNA testing and the reliability of the results depend — as with any other science — on good laboratory practice. Therefore, the continuity and authenticity of sample materials, including before they reach the laboratory, proper laboratory procedures during the many stages of testing, and the inclusion of control samples, are all necessary to ensure reliable results on which the scientist will ultimately base his conclusions.

In addition to assessing whether DNA profiles have been reliably produced from the relevant test materials, the scientist must reach a decision whether or not a match has been established. When a match is found, he will have to make an appropriate statistical evaluation of the results as evidence towards identity, using databases representative of the appropriate population to provide accurate assessments of fragment frequencies. Ultimately, the court will have to use the DNA results together with the other evidence in the case to reach a conclusion concerning guilt or innocence.

PART 2 — Legal issues

Graham Cooke
Barrister specialising in criminal work, Chambers of Michael Lawson QC, London

Deoxyribonucleic acid (DNA) evidence is very important and powerful; it proves a person did *not* commit a crime, rather than proves that he did. The figures presented by Patrick Lincoln show that, if an individual is outside the limits, he cannot have committed the crime or, in a parentage case, cannot be the father. The matching limits, whatever they may be, vary from laboratory to laboratory (accurate measurements are not possible); for example, the Metropolitan Police Forensic Science Laboratory uses a different margin of error for its measurement error than the Home Office. Whilst it is accepted that the *whole* DNA profile is unique to an individual (except for identical twins), it is nevertheless vital to realise that when the two, three or four particular positions on the DNA profile are pulled out and two bands taken from each, they might 'match' with those from another person. Such a match, though, does *not* prove that the profiles come from the same man or woman.

The use of the term DNA 'finger-printing' is to be deplored. It is up to all who do this sort of work to make sure that we understand what it means.

Lawyers generally are not numerate; judges, who were lawyers before they became judges, are therefore not numerate; jurors often can have trouble reading the oath — and are not usually excluded by that difficulty. The defence no longer has a right of challenge, and a juror can try a DNA case even though he could not read the oath.

All the scientists have a major task: how to get over their information, their particular expertise, their opinions to the court? It has to be worked at — I have now spent some three and a half years working on DNA cases. I have a mathematical background that makes it easier for me but, in a strange way, makes it more difficult for me to understand other people's difficulties. This is common when you are an expert in your own field. If I may offer some advice, talk to your family and other people about issues to try to get some feedback. In Lincoln's Inn, experts come to work with pupils in their advocacy lessons, and it is the *experts* who ask us afterwards how well they performed. It is interesting to see the differences; we have to be tactful sometimes because some are good and others not.

DNA: the legal position

A sample (eg bloodstain or semen) taken from the scene of the crime must obviously be kept in as good a condition as possible because it will eventually be matched with blood from a suspect, or the readings from that blood. If the suspect is not excluded, the next question that has to be answered is 'What does this mean?'. It means, in fact, that the individual is not excluded, and therefore the results are *consistent with...* This is the point made by Judge Stephens (page 6): the expert says it is *consistent with* his being the attacker, the perpetrator.

How will this help a jury? It has to be put in some sort of meaningful terms to the jury. It does not mean that the scientist can say 'This is the man' — whether it is one in a million, one in 40 million or one in 100 million who have that particular profile. It is not the scientist's job to say this. It is not a matter of rule of law; it is a matter of logic. The scientist is not in a position to say '*That* semen came from *that* man'.

The prosecutor's fallacy

A situation known as the 'prosecutor's fallacy'[1,2] has occurred in a number of important cases, which are only now coming through the Court of Appeal. It arises where the judge has misstated the evidence to the jury because neither he nor the lawyers have understood it — and, I regret to say, there have been occasions when the forensic scientists did not seem to understand either.

The proposition — in general terms, not specifically in relation to DNA — is as follows: if the perpetrator of a crime is known to be, say, left-handed and to wear glasses and, for the sake of argument, it is also known that one in ten of the population wears glasses and one in five is left-handed then, assuming these two characteristics are independent of each other, two in a hundred people will wear glasses and be left-handed. If this were relevant in a trial — or any other issue — it is a simple proposition to explain to the jury: 'It is two in a hundred; what a coincidence that *this* man, who has been picked up down the street near the crime happens to be left-handed and he wears glasses'.

The prosecutor's fallacy consists in presenting this to the jury as being 50 to 1 'on' that he was the man who did it, because of those two pieces of evidence. Put in those terms, it seems unbelievable that somebody would perpetrate this view.

The reason why DNA has such a good — in fact, overstated —

reputation in proving guilt or identity is because of the largeness of the figures. We read about one in a million, and I have even seen one in 800 million. If you have a suspect for a crime and look, not at his whole DNA but at the DNA fragments that we are talking about, and the database throws up statistics of one in 800 million, it is tempting to say 'That is so powerful — what does it mean?', and then, 'It must mean that he is guilty of the crime' — and so we get drawn into overstating the case — the prosecutor's fallacy.

The statisticians and those working in probability logic are the experts in this — which comes back to Judge Stephens' point (page 3) that the expertise of the forensic scientist is in doing all the extremely complicated, difficult technical work to get to the stage at which we have the X-ray showing these bands. Thereafter, some computer expertise is needed for the database (it is all statistics) and some logic to explain the results to the jury.

I hope that what I have described has opened some eyes in terms of the use of DNA in the criminal court.

Legislation and DNA

The change in legislation now going through is enormously important in terms of civil liberties because there is to be a DNA data bank of people's (usually criminals') DNA, as defined using three or four probes. The prosecution (I suppose I ought to say 'we' and include all of us) will be able to look at that data bank and see whether there is a match with the DNA profile of the suspect. If there is, it will be argued that this individual must have carried out the crime — without there necessarily being any other evidence.

This is the potential position we may reach. Before this happens, DNA profiling has to get better than it is now — not just on the technological and measurement sides but also on the statistical side. A professor of statistics, an expert in this area, told me that he deplores the lack of professionalism involved on the statistical side of DNA: it is dreadful, it is not up to 'O' level statistics. Some forensic scientists are in love with the technology of it, and think that it *does* provide proof of guilt. It is important that the technology and statistics develop sufficiently to allow *effective* proof that an accused 'is the man' — but this is in the future, and we are not there yet.

The role of the defence counsel

I want to deal with the role of the defence barrister and solicitor (I include defence solicitors here because they have the same duty).

It is our job, within the rules of court and the proper procedures, to do everything possible on behalf of our defendant. If he says 'I didn't do it', whether the chances that he did not are one in 800 million or whatever, it is our job to accept that (or whatever other 'unlikely' story he might tell us) as the truth, to work with it and do everything we can. If this means cross-examining a prosecution expert witness 'into the ground', that is our job.

In criminal procedures the defence does not have to call its own expert — this is different from the civil procedures. I can go into court and put propositions to the prosecution without having to disclose my expert's report. I am not there to prove the defendant innocent; I am not there to work on the balance of probabilities — but if I create a doubt in the jury's mind about that evidence or about the whole issue, that is enough to get an acquittal.

Finally, I will ask any expert on anything — not just DNA — whether he could be wrong. You might ponder how you would answer this question. Whatever the answer, I will then ask whether he has been wrong on other occasions. Since I always look at all the prosecution working papers anyway, it may be unnecessary to ask if I can see all the drafts of the expert's report, but you might consider from the civil experience (page 14) that we should ask this question — an overlooked transcription error is not unknown and may be crucial. Those drafts would be disclosable, certainly in criminal cases. In my view, this is the only way to defend cases — and that is our duty.

References

1. *R v. Deen* [1994], Cr. App. R. 566.
2. *R v. Gordon* [1995], 2 Gr. App. R. 61.

Limitations of psychiatric evidence

Nigel Eastman
Head, Section of Forensic Psychiatry, St George's Hospital Medical School, London

This chapter is written from the perspective of an academic and clinician who has considerable experience of both civil and criminal litigation. The subject, limitations of psychiatric evidence, immediately suggests a distinction between limitations *as they are* and limitations *as they should be*. Another distinction which may be drawn is between those limitations which arise from the philosophy and practice of psychiatry as a discipline *per se* and those which arise from the interface between psychiatry and the law. Both these distinctions apply, in fact, to all branches of medicine. However, there is something unique about the relationship between the law and psychiatry, by contrast with other medical specialties.

In *An essay concerning human understanding*,[1] John Locke observed that ' "person" is a forensic term'. Coming from the opposite direction, a 19th century lawyer, Sir James Stephens, wrote:

What is the meaning of the word 'mind'? What is a sane and what is an insane mind? Difficult and remote from law as these enquiries may be, it is impossible to deal with the subject at all without entering into some extent upon the discussion.[2]

Hence, via the philosophy of mind, psychiatry and law are intimately intertwined.

Differences between psychiatric and other medical expertise

The preceding quotations emphasise a fundamental difference between the use in court of psychiatric expertise and the use of other medical expertise. The difference arises essentially because psychiatry deals with the same 'stuff' as does the law, in terms of its ultimate issues. The courts are frequently interested, within their own terms, in psychology, behaviour and intention, and — albeit directed towards different purposes — so is psychiatry.[3] There is, therefore, much closer coherence of topic interest between law and psychiatry than between, for example, law and forensic pathology. The 'stuff' of forensic pathology is, after all, physical, and in this it frequently differs from psychiatry. It certainly differs from the direct content and interest of the law. The law is interested in forensic pathological evidence only as one step on the road to determining intention and culpability.

Boundary problems

I make the latter point because this merging of interest between law and psychiatry gives rise to 'boundary problems'. For example, the psychiatrist is standing in the witness box at the Old Bailey and is asked by defence counsel, in relation to Section 2 of the Homicide Act 1957, 'Doctor, does this man suffer from "diminished responsibility"?'. This term is of course not listed in either the World Health Organisation (WHO) International Classification of Diseases (ICD) or the American Psychiatric Association's Diagnostic and Statistical Manual (DSM). However, there is clearly the immediate potential for movement from psychiatric ground straight into legal ground. It is crucially important to keep clear the boundary between the two and to resist such migration. It is more difficult to keep this boundary in forensic psychiatric practice than in other branches of medicine.

The different approaches of psychiatry and the law

The difficulties that arise in psychiatric practice in the courts occur not only because there is coherence of interest between law and psychiatry but because the two disciplines come at the issues through completely different epistemologies and modes of thought. The difficulty for the psychiatrist, in both civil and criminal courts, is that he has to fit psychiatric concepts of disorder and disease into legal definitions. There is, in effect, a psychiatric diagnosis set alongside some legal concept — for example, 'insanity' or 'abnormality of mind' — and the psychiatrist is asked to fit the one into the other.

The legal 'fictional' approach

These construct disparities arise out of the very different purposes of psychiatry and the law. Psychiatry is concerned with the investigation and diagnosis of mental disorder; more specific purposes of diagnosis include taxonomy, prognosis, treatment and the understanding of psychopathology. In comparison, the law's purpose is directed towards moral judgments and is heavily value-laden. It is also essentially 'fictional' in its approach: it constructs fictional notions for its own purposes. Take, for example, the terms 'insanity', 'disease of the mind', 'abnormality of the mind' or even 'psychopathic disorder' in Section 1 of the Mental Health Act. They *look* medical but are not; they are definitions *constructed by the law*. As a result, although they often seem connected with medicine they look peculiar from a medical perspective.

As an example, I will paraphrase what Lord Denning said in a famous case called *Bratty v. A-G for Northern Ireland*.[4] He stated that a 'disease of the mind' was something which resulted in violence and was prone to recur. He elaborated this view by saying that it was, at least, the sort of 'disease' for which somebody should be 'locked up' (he did not put it quite like that). It is clear what Denning has done. He has in mind somebody who, for example, has epilepsy (or some other medical condition) and who has been violent, and he takes the view that it would not be good for society were such a person to be at large. He therefore defines 'disease of the mind' specifically so as to achieve a social purpose. In so doing he adopts a peculiar definition which has little to do with medicine.

Interesting situations can arise as a result of the legal fictional approach: for example, several fictions may potentially apply to one particular situation. A defendant charged with murder may have a defence under 'diminished responsibility' in terms of Section 2 of the Homicide Act 1957, a defence under 'insanity' in terms of the McNaghten rules and, because she is a mother who has killed her child within a year of its birth, she may be charged with infanticide instead of murder. In different circumstances, there might be the legal possibility of pleading the 'provocation' defence within Section 3 of the Homicide Act alongside the 'diminished responsibility' defence. This latter combination is particularly peculiar. The defence is saying to the jury, either the defendant was an entirely reasonable person who was provoked by the extraordinarily unreasonable behaviour of the victim *or* he is mentally abnormal. Psychiatry must try to fit its own 'real' diagnoses about real psychiatric conditions into these various, and sometimes mutually contradictory, legal fictions.

Normality and 'the reasonable man'

The criminal courts also have notions of 'normality'. They presume both rationality and that the accused intended, unless there is good evidence to the contrary, to do what he did in a 'normal' way. There is also a legal fictional personality, 'the reasonable man' (the law has not been good at recognising 'the reasonable woman'!), otherwise

identified as 'the man on the Clapham omnibus'. He is a sort of cor-
porate or aggregate personality, embodying all facets of reasonable
or predictable behaviour within a society of individuals. In reality, of
course, no one individual holds all those characteristics. There are
at any moment many men on the Clapham omnibus but no one of
them is *the* man on the Clapham omnibus. The role of psychiatry in
the criminal courts as regards verdict is potentially to rebut the pre-
sumption of rationality or ordinary intentionality in one way or
another. However, it is important to re-emphasise the extraordinary
difficulty for psychiatry, when dealing with matters so close to the
law's own discipline, in avoiding being sucked into matters which
are none of its business. The psychiatrist must resist answering the
question, 'Doctor, is this man "diminished"?'.

Specific problems for psychiatry in the courts

In moving from the general to the particular I shall deal only with
verdict issues, although 'fitness to plead', reliability of police interviews, 'suggestibility' and sentencing are other important areas.
Section 2 of the Homicide Act (to which I have already referred)
illustrates well the sorts of problems which arise when psychiatry
goes into the courts. Section 2 states that murder may be reduced to
manslaughter, *first*, if the defendant had:

> an abnormality of mind (whether arising from a condition of
> arrested or retarded development of mind or any inherent cause
> or induced by disease or injury).

The parenthetic clause restricts the phrase 'abnormality of
mind': an individual cannot be abnormal of mind just by virtue of
being angry.
Secondly, it is necessary that the abnormality was such as substan-
tially to impair the person's mental responsibility.

The 'two limbs' of Section 2.

Forensic psychiatrists make a distinction (as do lawyers) between
what may be called the 'first limb' and the 'second limb' of Section
2. The first limb, 'abnormality of mind' with the attached parenthetic clause, sounds rather medical. The second limb, 'substantial
impairment of mental responsibility', does not sound at all medical;
rather, it sounds entirely moral, ethical and legal.
Consideration of these two limbs is instructive about the relationship between psychiatry and law more generally. What is an

'abnormality of mind'? In a case called *R v. Byrne,*[5] the court decided that it was a condition so different from the ordinary person that the reasonable man would consider it to be abnormal. We are back to the man on the Clapham omnibus, this time asking his view from the jury box.

The latter definition is an extraordinarily broad one, allowing for extremely wide variation in the types of medical evidence of disorder which doctors may choose to put before the courts. Hence, some doctors are not prepared to say that there was an abnormality of mind unless delusions or hallucinations were present, whereas others are prepared to say that there was such an abnormality solely on the basis that the defendant had suffered an 'adjustment reaction'. Adjustment reaction is, of course, an accepted diagnostic term in the WHO ICD 10. However, the observed variation in expert practice raises the question of what sort of constraints, if any, should be put on psychiatric evidence in defining the presence or absence of legal abnormality of mind.

Clearly there is an inherent problem relating to abnormality of mind in what might be termed 'spectrum disorder' cases. Hence, there may be no clear categorical definition of disorder. For example, a depressive illness may be seen properly to lie on a spectrum: it can be extremely severe — you die because you do not drink — or so mild that it amounts almost to normal sadness, merely a reaction to a life stressor. This causes enormous problems in the courts because, again, doctors differ as to the level of illness on that spectrum they consider is required for a depressive illness to count as abnormality of mind. Also, at the bottom end of this spectrum of disorder it may indeed be difficult to make a clear distinction between normality and abnormality.

Similar arguments frequently arise in court in relation to personality disorder. The disorder itself is, by definition, a spectrum disorder because the abnormality is demonstrated by comparison with a normal population, not by comparison with the person's own previous 'normality' — the person *never was* normal.

The 'second' limb of Section 2.

Returning specifically to the second limb of Section 2, ultimately, this should not be any concern of doctors — substantial impairment of mental responsibility is not taught in medical schools as a diagnostic entity. A doctor can properly define abnormal mental states (as best retrospective reconstruction allows), and also say something about the way in which the person's perception, judgment or volition is likely to have been affected. However, he should resist the final step of saying'... and therefore there was substantial impairment of mental responsibility'. Rather, he should define in medical terms the abnormality of the defendant's mental state at the time of the alleged offence and allow the court to take that final step. This represents a real distinction, but it is a fine one and sometimes gives rise to difficulty. Such difficulty is illustrated by the following (not uncommon) courtroom exchange:

> *Defence lawyer to psychiatrist:* Doctor, is this man diminished?

> *Psychiatrist to judge:* My Lord, could I ask for your direction on this? Is that not, with respect, a question ultimately for the jury and not for me to answer?

> *Judge to psychiatrist:* Quite right, Doctor — now would you answer the question?

The courts are not consistent in the application of their own rules of evidence and, in fact, may wrongly apply the rules relating to expert evidence. The psychiatrist must therefore be vigilant against assisting in something which is legally and, I would suggest, ethically wrong.

Other difficulties arise in relation to the second limb when, for example, at the time of the killing a defendant suffered from a depressive illness or a severe personality disorder, but was also drunk or on drugs at the time of the offence. How is it possible to answer the inevitable (and legally required) hypothetical question, 'Doctor, if he had not been drunk, would it have happened?'? Being self intoxicated is not (except in very rare circumstances) a defence; there is therefore the theoretical legal need to attribute causation between the two factors. However, in practice it is obviously impossible to re-run events and determine whether the illness (or personality disorder) would have been a sufficient cause of the behaviour in the absence of alcohol or drugs.

The defence of provocation

The alternative legal defence of provocation, within Section 3 of the Homicide Act 1957, is also not without its problems. In psychiatric or psychological reality, a large number of homicide (especially domestic homicide) cases sit properly somewhere between the poles of diminished responsibility and provocation. However, such a 'mid point' is not legally permissible. Legal defences are discrete entities. The classic case is that of a husband who is rejected by his wife, perhaps finds out about her lover, and who develops a moderately severe depressive illness which involves both a mood disturbance and some biological symptoms. One night, his wife says something provocative, such as 'You're terrible in bed, he's much better'. He loses control and kills her. Is the proper (potential) defence diminished responsibility or provocation? In psychological reality there is a mixture of both. Indeed, this may be one reason why defence counsel sometimes run diminished responsibility and provocation side-by-side. It appears irrational, but it is done in the hope that the jury will effectively come to some judicial average, even though, theoretically, they are supposed to decide specifically which of two mutually exclusive defences they accept.

Limitations of method

Leaving aside particular legal defences, forensic psychiatry is subject to general limitations of method. Clearly, one great difficulty is that it assesses defendants retrospectively; it tries to reconstruct a mental state sometimes up to a year after the event. Another problem is the amount of reliance necessarily placed upon what the defendant says. Hence, when appearing for the defence, a classic gambit by the Crown is to observe, 'Doctor, you're just basing your opinion on what the defendant told you, aren't you?'. This is true to some extent, but there are certain ways of properly rebutting such an attack. Clearly, if a defendant displays a syndrome which represents a recognisable diagnostic jigsaw of signs and symptoms, this in itself tends to validate the conclusion — unless you think that the defendant has looked up the details in a medical textbook and fed you a composite lie. Suggesting to the defendant symptoms which do *not* fit the diagnosis may also test reliability. Further, there will often be access to large amounts of information beyond the defendant, such as depositions and taped police interviews, which were established roughly contemporaneously with the crime. It may also be possible to interview other people who, if they do not have a vested interest in the outcome of the case, may be useful in the attempt to reconstruct the defendant's state of mind at the time. There also may be medical records.

Aside from problems of diagnostic validation, it is perhaps not surprising that there is sometimes variation between psychiatrists in what they say in the criminal courts about certain sorts of cases which arises out of difference of diagnostic approach. In his book on Denis Neilson,[6,7] Masters nicknamed one of the three eminent forensic psychiatrists who gave evidence 'Dr No', because it was said that he simply answered 'No' cryptically to a large number of the questions he was asked. By contrast, another doctor, who was both a forensic psychiatrist and a psychoanalyst, went into enormous detail about Neilson's psychopathology. It is difficult for the courts when different experts appear to adopt such fundamentally different approaches. However, if all the psychiatrists in a criminal case were on a ward round they would probably mostly agree about the nature of the defendant. Because of the approach of the law, not only opinions but also methods become polarised in the witness box.

In order to minimise differences of approach, there is one crucial quality standard towards which psychiatry should, in my view, strive. No argument regarding mental illness or disorder should be put forward without reference to one of the two accepted international classification systems of diseases, the ICD or the DSM. This would protect the courts, both civil and criminal, from idiosyncratic diagnoses. It would also improve the reliability and consistency of individual doctors. Further, areas of disagreement would be reduced or, where they were inherent, the bases of different opinions would be made explicit, enabling the court to decide which approach it wished to accept.

It is important, therefore, for psychiatrists to define clearly not only their opinions but also the evidence and theoretical approach upon which those opinions are based.

Civil litigation

Let me turn briefly to civil litigation, and specifically to negligence actions involving psychiatric injury. If there is physical injury to a plaintiff which should have been within the foresight of the defendant, if it was caused by the defendant's careless action, and if all the other requirements of the tort of negligence are satisfied, it is possible for the plaintiff to gain additional damages for any consequential psychiatric injury. However, where there is solely psychiatric injury the courts apply unusual legal restrictions upon the circumstances in which a plaintiff can recover damages.[8-10]

'Nervous shock'

Problems arise for plaintiffs where there is no physical injury but solely (to use the legal term) 'nervous shock'. This is an area in which recent so-called 'disaster cases' have given rise to much attempted legal development. One such development has been the entering of claims not only by victims physically present at any disaster but also by relatives of those victims who have witnessed the disaster, usually through the medium of television. So far, such claims have been unsuccessful, even though the psychiatric injury is valid.[9]

A further problem for plaintiffs arising from the legal definition of nervous shock is that the psychiatric injury — which, quite properly, must derive from a recognised psychiatric diagnosis and not from mere mental distress — must arise, as it were, as a 'sudden event' and not through a prolonged process. There must have been a 'shock'. This is psychiatrically unreal.[8]

Finally, even when a recognised psychiatric diagnosis and a sudden event are established, it may be difficult to prove causation. For example, where there is a depressive illness, an expert may be able to point merely to a temporal relationship between the litigated event and the illness, alongside the absence of any other clear precipitating factors. This may not always be a strong basis upon which to rely in order to establish causation. Similar problems can occur even in cases involving coincidental psychiatric and physical injury (that is, not legal 'nervous shock').

Post-traumatic stress disorder

If the claimed psychiatric injury arises from post-traumatic stress disorder (PTSD) this may present less of a problem in regard to causation.[10] Here causation may often be inferred by the content of the symptomatology, which may relate directly to the event. The 're-experiencing' and 'avoidance' symptoms of PTSD may suggest causation by being directly reflective of the litigated event.

However, a different medico-legal problem may potentially be on the horizon in regard to PTSD if, as postulated by some psychiatrists, the current *objective* definition of 'criterion A' (that the other PTSD symptoms arose from a 'life threatening' traumatic event which was 'terrifying') becomes inessential to the diagnosis — that is, if the severity of the *subjective* meaning of a stressor is all that need be addressed in determining the presence of criterion A. The law has rules concerning the 'forseeability' of harm arising, and a defendant cannot be held liable if he could not have predicted the harm from the trauma.

An analogy

To end on a much lighter note, when I teach junior doctors about going to court I illustrate the general relationship between law and medicine by use of an analogy. It is a particularly appropriate analogy for psychiatry because, as I suggested at the beginning, what the specialty addresses is so close to the very things in which the courts are themselves directly legally interested (in terms of thought, intention and so on). It seems to me that going into court is a little like being sent in to open the batting in cricket for England against the West Indies. You take guard and see the bowler hurtling down towards you from the other end. He releases the ball and, as it is in flight, you realise that it is in fact, a *rugby* ball. You survive the first delivery and immediately go across to the umpire and say, 'Excuse me, this isn't cricket'. The umpire replies, 'Absolutely right. We call it rugby cricket, we rather enjoy it, it's quite fun'. You then complain, 'You seem rather to be on their side', to which he replies, 'Yes, I suppose that's right — I mean it's *our* game. We play it all the time and sometimes we invite somebody else to come in and have a bat'. You respond, 'Well, I'm not used to batting rugby balls'. Finally the umpire insists, 'Of course, but now please go back to the crease'.

References

1. Locke J. *An essay concerning human understanding.* New York: Dover, 1959: Book 2, Ch 27.

2. Stephen, Sir J. *A history of the criminal law of England,* vol 2. London: Macmillan, 1883.

3. Eastman NLG. Psychiatric, psychological and legal models of man. In: Peay J, Shapland J, eds. *International Journal of Law and Psychiatry* (special edn) 1992;**15**:157–69.

4. *Bratty v. A-G for Northern Ireland* [1963] AC 386; [1961] 3 WLR 965; [1961] 3 All ER 523.

5. *R v. Byrne* [1960] 2 QB 396; [1960] 3 WLR 440; [1960] 3 All ER 1.

6. Masters B. *Killing for company.* London: Cape, 1985.

7. Masters B. *Killing for company.* London: Hodder & Stoughton, 1986.

8. Eastman NLG. *Legal fiction and psychological reality.* Hardwicke Lecture, Lincoln's Inn, 1995 (as yet unpublished).

9. Napier M. Civil law and psychiatric injury. In: Black D, Newman M, Mezey G, *et al,* eds. *Psychological trauma: a developmental approach.* London: Gaskell, 1995 (in press).

10. Eastman NLG. Assessing for psychiatric damages and 'nervous shock'. *Advances in Psychiatric Treatment* 1995;**1**:no.6.

6 Pathological evidence

Stephen Leadbeatter

Senior Lecturer in Forensic Pathology, Wales Institute of Forensic Medicine, University of Wales College of Medicine, Institute of Pathology, Cardiff Royal Infirmary

It appears a common misconception among the legal profession that the forensic pathologist is a scientist: 'You are going to give us the scientific evidence, Doctor'. One of the definitions of 'science' in the *Shorter Oxford English Dictionary* reads:

> A branch of study which is concerned either with a connected body of demonstrated truths or with observed facts systematically classified and more or less colligated by being brought under general laws, and which includes trustworthy methods for the discovery of new truth within its own domain.

Demonstrated truths

The only common ground shared by forensic pathology and that definition of science is a *body*, which may be connected in some cases but not in others. What in forensic pathology can be regarded as *demonstrated truths*? The fundamental question to which the forensic pathologist is believed to supply the answer is 'What is the cause of death?'. An opinion as to cause of death may involve unstated assumption; in strict truth, it is not possible to say with certainty exactly how or of what a person died — unless the individual giving this opinion personally effected the death of an individual under precise physiological monitoring. The opinion given relates to diseases or conditions *with* which the individual died, which are not necessarily the same as the condition *from* which the individual died.

Consider a case where the post-mortem examination reveals only significant coronary artery atherosclerosis without acute complication, but where someone has admitted having strangled the victim with a soft ligature. In the absence of knowledge of that admission, the cause of death may be given as 'coronary artery atherosclerosis'. The pathologist cannot deny either that the degree of disease demonstrated may exist in the asymptomatic living or that death may result from the application of pressure on the neck by means of a soft ligature without evidence being seen at post-mortem examination *once the ligature has been removed.* From the *positive* objective pathological evidence alone, the cause of death remains 'coronary artery atherosclerosis'. Given knowledge — or even an awareness of the possibility — of the admitted application of pressure on the neck, the cause of death is better given, from a summation of the positive and *negative* pathological evidence (and an awareness of a practical problem!), as 'indeterminate'.

Such a case is perhaps more complex than that in which there are *no* findings at the post-mortem examination — when there should be no intellectual objection to a designation of the cause of death as 'unascertained'. When first encountered, such causes of death pose apparent difficulty to the legal profession, but that is — if real — a matter for the lawyer, *not* for the pathologist.

The forensic pathologist must also be aware of the potential problem with findings at post-mortem examination encapsulated in this following fictional interchange:

> *Barrister:* Tell me, Doctor, from your experience, would the injuries you observed prove fatal?

> *Pathologist (with asperity):* Of course they would — as a pathologist, I have experience *only* of fatal cases.

The forensic pathologist must acknowledge that there is a spectrum of clinical incapacity arising from the injury which he has demonstrated, and must not assume that death is the only possible outcome simply because the dead are the material in which he demonstrates that injury.

Observed facts

Demonstrated truths may therefore be illusory. What about *observed facts* and their *systematic classification?* Consider first, an admission made by an alleged assailant regarding how a victim was killed: does that assailant *know* precisely what happened? Could it be that, in circumstances of stress, the ability to function as an objective witness, whose later accounts of actions are considered to be of unassailable veracity and resistant to outside influence, is open to question?

There are also problems implicit in the medico-legal tag: 'In your (my) experience, ...'. What, in truth, can be said regarding the experience of a forensic pathologist in matters of violent death? It is — presumably — both aleatory and vicarious; if 'observation' is substituted for 'experience', it remains aleatory and influenced by age and geography. It is inevitable — and entirely laudable — that the pathologist should seek assistance from the literature relating to the injury demonstrated at his examination. But here are additional problems, as may be exemplified by the questions which arise in the investigation of a case of 'traumatic basal subarachnoid haemorrhage'. Critical consideration of an incident of blunt impact believed to have given rise to subarachnoid haemorrhage demands answers to the following:

- What is the precise source of the bleeding?

- Does injury to a blood vessel result from the blunt impact itself?

- Does injury to a blood vessel result, not from direct impact, but from movement of the head on the neck as a consequence of the impact?

- If injury to a blood vessel may result from such movement, may it not result from a movement of the head on the neck in an attempt to *avoid* impact?

- Might not injury to a blood vessel result from another impact or movement of the head on the neck occurring during a fall to the ground engendered by the initial impact?

- What is the time period between an impact which is regarded as having caused injury to a blood vessel and subsequent collapse?

- What is the capacity for movement of the victim during that period?

The literature

The search in the literature for answers to these questions raises further questions regarding the literature itself:

Problems of language

Is any literature available and, if there is, is it in a language which the pathologist can interpret? The language may be that of a different country or of a different medical specialty. Can the pathologist be confident that he and, say, the paediatrician or neurosurgeon are, in fact, 'speaking the same language'? Are there circumstances in the latter specialties which may be implicit in their 'jargon', but which the pathologist fails to appreciate, given that he is outside his field of expertise, and therefore misinterprets the data?

It is easy for the pathologist to fail to realise that, for example, a paediatrician may form the opinion that an injury is non-accidental in aetiology not so much, perhaps, from the injury itself but from knowledge of the 'milestones of development' of an infant or child and comparison of those 'milestones' with a 'carer's' account of how the injury was sustained. The paediatrician will be aware from personal interviews with the 'carer' of any variation or inconsistency in such accounts, which will be important in any process of decision making — as detailed, for example, by Duhaime *et al*[1] regarding the aetiology of injury.

Problems of truths and facts

When literature exists and can be understood, how can the reader be confident that the details given by the author are free from the difficulties noted in the above discussion of *demonstrated truths* and *observed facts*?

Consideration of these questions in the light of the given definition of 'science' in the *Shorter Oxford English Dictionary* demonstrates again that forensic pathology is *not* a science —

> which includes trustworthy methods for the discovery of new truth within its own domain.

The ethical and legal barriers to the testing of hypotheses concerning mechanisms of injury and their quantification are evident; nor should the pathologist be seduced into thinking that the (subjectively) appropriate outcome of legal proceedings is a substitute for scientific validation of whatever hypothesis or explanation has been advanced. These limitations are by no means exclusive to forensic pathology but apply to all medical specialties concerned with the causation of trauma. Recognition of these limitations may explain the absence of detail encountered when seeking answers in the literature to such specific questions as posed above.

The basis of expert opinion

What, then, is the basis of 'expert opinion' and what is its relation to 'evidence'? Definitions of 'opinion' in the *Shorter Oxford English Dictionary*, although stating precisely what has been argued, appear disturbing in the criminal context of 'beyond a reasonable doubt':

What one opines; judgment resting on grounds insufficient for complete demonstration; belief of something as probable or as seeming to one's own mind to be true.

The formal statement by an expert or professional man of what he thinks, judges or advises upon a matter submitted to him.

The potential for bias, albeit unwitting, is obvious: how can the professional man be satisfied of the completeness, relevance and veracity of the *matter submitted to him?* To what degree will his opinion be coloured by the evidence of others rather than be an objective conclusion drawn from his evidence alone? And yet, to allow opinion as to the consistency of the expert evidence with allegations, knowledge of those allegations and other relevant statements is essential.

Are the tags 'on the balance of probabilities' in civil proceedings and 'beyond a reasonable doubt' in criminal cases applicable to the 'expert opinion' *in isolation,* rather than to the totality of the evidence? Both involve a quantification of the weight of the evidence upon which the opinion is based which, as has been discussed above, cannot be substantiated in many cases. Even were that substantiation considered possible, how can it be said where an *individual case* would lie within a *statistical series* of similar cases and, therefore, how can the degree of probability be given?

The solution appears to lie in careful use of the neutral terms 'possible' and 'consistent' and in an unwillingness to go beyond a description of the parameters allowed by the expert evidence, thereby leaving conclusions to be drawn *by the jury* in criminal cases or *by the judge* in, for example, child abuse cases in the civil court, in the light of *all the evidence.*

A judicial review of the expert

These arguments appear to be in accord with judgments given in child cases:

The expert should not mislead by omissions. He should consider all the material facts in reaching his conclusions and must not omit to consider the material facts which could detract from his concluded opinion.

If experts look for and report on factors which tend to support a particular proposition or case, their reports should still ... be properly researched.

If the expert's opinion is not properly researched because he considers that insufficient data are available, then he must say so and indicate that his opinion is no more than a provisional one.[2]

The expert formed an assessment and expressed his opinion within the particular area of his expertise. The judge decided particular issues in individual cases. It was therefore not for the judge to become involved in medical controversy except in the extremely rare case where such a controversy was itself an issue in the case and a judicial assessment of it became necessary for the proper resolution of the proceedings.

The dependence of the court on the skill, knowledge and, above all, the professional and intellectual integrity of the expert witness could not be overemphasised. The judge's task was difficult enough as it was in sensitive children's cases.[3]

Given the acknowledgement in legal commentary on child abuse cases in the civil courts that

the standard of proof in such proceedings may vary depending on the gravity of the issue to be resolved, the consequences which may ensue if it is proved and the particular facts of a given case[4]

it is easy to appreciate the difficulty of the judicial task and the necessity for careful choice of language when defining the parameters of the state of knowledge upon which the expert's opinion is based.

The strenuous cross-examination which may follow from the approach discussed should be no bar to the acknowledgement of the limitations of an opinion based upon objective pathological evidence.

References

1. Duhaime AC, Alario AJ, Lewander WJ, Schut L, *et al*. Head injury in very young children: mechanisms, injury types, and ophthalmologic findings in 100 hospitalized patients younger than 2 years of age. *Pediatrics* 1992;**90**:179–85.
2. *Re R (a minor)* (expert's evidence) (Note) [1991] 1FLR 291.
3. *Re AB (a minor)* (medical issues: expert evidence) [1994] TLR, 17 August.
4. Lyon C, de Cruz P. *Child abuse*, 2nd edn. Bristol: Family Law, 1993.

7 Forensic dentistry

David K Whittaker

Reader in Oral Biology and Consultant, Dental School, University of Wales College of Medicine, Cardiff

> *Expert:* one with special knowledge or skill causing him to be an authority. A specialist. To know by experience.

Whilst forensic pathology is a recognised specialty within the discipline of medicine, forensic odontology or forensic dentistry is not recognised as such by the General Dental Council or by the profession in general in the UK. There is no formal training in forensic dentistry in the UK, although, by nature of their experience, a handful of people have become known as forensic odontologists. Perhaps, then, one of the most serious limitations of expert evidence within the field of forensic dentistry is to define who is a forensic dentist?

Who is a dental expert?

Who or what is an expert? So far as the court is concerned, a qualified dental surgeon may be viewed as the most appropriate person to advise on matters concerning the teeth and the oral structures. This may well be true if the issues are of a clinical nature involving previous treatment, trauma or future expectations, but in the context of forensic dentistry the dentist is required to give opinion in two main areas.

Identification

The first area is largely to do with identification in all its forms, identification of fragments as well as of people, and may involve determination of age, sex, specific dental features, facial features and comparison with dental records.

Teeth marks

The other half of the practice of forensic dentistry is the application of the teeth as weapons as they inflict bite marks.

The majority of dentists in practice in the UK will never have identified a putrescent or traumatised human body or have dealt with a bite mark. Moreover, they will almost certainly never have appeared in court. Is such an individual a satisfactory expert? He may well be justified as such because of his general dental training and experience, but if he were to be asked 'How many cases of this nature have you seen and dealt with, and in how many of them have you appeared in court?', the answer may well be informative. Colleagues regarded as national authorities, who have been justified as such in the courts, will admit that they have actually appeared in only a handful of cases.

There are thus two main areas of difficulty in relation to the dental expert:

- his direct expertise in the matters before the court; and,

- his experience — or lack of it — in giving evidence in the unfamiliar surroundings of the court.

Scientific limitations

Like all aspects of medicine, dentistry is a complex mixture of science and art. As far as age and developmental changes in the teeth and surrounding structures are concerned, the biological principles have been understood for most of this century. There is an extensive literature concerning the sequence of events, and published data on the expected status of development of the deciduous and permanent dentitions through to the eruption and completion of the last teeth to develop (the permanent third molars). By looking, for example, at the extent of root development (Figure 1), any competent dentist might be expected to be able to determine the age at which an individual died.

However, consider the statistics of the situation: the author of the research data on which the forensic opinion is to be based may well have examined thousands of developing teeth. He may have produced statistical standard deviations which are available to the court — but who is to say whether the case in question lies within those statistical parameters or is the one in a million lying well outside them? The expert in court may need the raw data of those thousands of teeth that have been examined, but such data are never

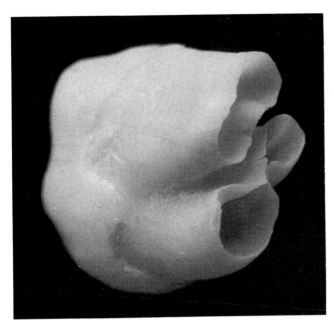

Fig 1. *Root development of third molar. The roots are incomplete and age determination depends upon their length.*

available. In a scientific sense, these are considerable limitations, and the expert may be able to give only a percentage likelihood of the particular age within the accepted range.

The problem becomes even more acute once the third molars have completed their development. One of the standard methods of determining age at death is to examine the extent of translucency of the root of the tooth (Figure 2). Dye infusion and computer mapping are now used to study this but, in reality, little is known of the biological variation inherent in this method.

Science becomes increasingly sophisticated, but there are limits of science even in apparently sophisticated methodology. Amino acids can now be extracted from the teeth and their left- or right-handedness examined. The ratio between these types of molecule is related accurately to the age of the individual. The expert will be aware that a putrefying body can produce a lack of precision in this determination, but he cannot say how frequently this occurs, what is its importance and what allowances should be made for it.

Computer technology has moved into the field of facial reconstruction in identification procedures, and it is now possible to reconstruct a facial likeness on the skull of a deceased person (Figure 3). The literature abounds with descriptions of artistic reconstructions, the use of computers and electronic imaging devices. The problem is that none of these has been tested in a

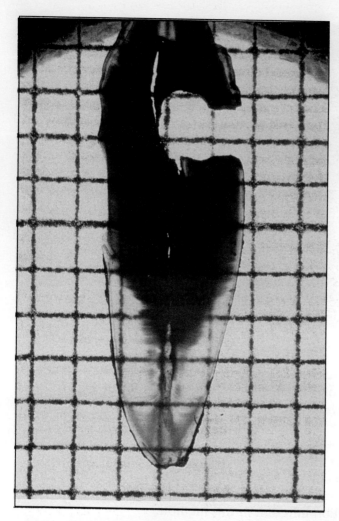

Fig 2.
Measurement of translucency at the root of a tooth. The 'sclerotic' clear area is related to the age of the individual.

double-blind fashion in the laboratory. The scientific methodology may look impressive in court but may also be extremely dubious.

Even the apparently straightforward dental record may be open to interpretation, and only rarely does the dental record made available to the expert match exactly the situation in the mouth of the deceased. What should be the position of the expert in relation to these discrepancies, and what should the defence or prosecution expert make of them? Individuals may make mistakes in writing the dental records. Do we know how frequently this happens? Patients may have had work completed after the record was written. Some of the discrepancies are compatible with the deceased being the same person as the individual whose records are produced in court, and some are incompatible. It behoves the expert to explain in detail to

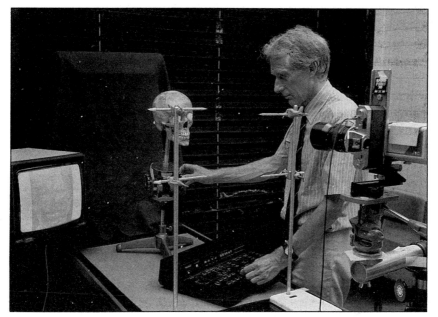

Fig 3. *The use of computer technology in facial reconstruction. Images of the face are electronically superimposed upon an image of the skull.*

the court where his limitations lie, and how far his opinion may be supported.

On the question of the teeth as weapons, the expert may be on even less safe ground. People generally do not like being bitten and tend to move out of the way. Also, they are frequently bitten on curved and soft tissues which bend and flex and change shape. The impression made by the teeth may be only partial, it may be moving, it may be of only one or two teeth. If the person survives, the tissues will undergo post-injury reaction such as swelling; if the individual is dead, putrefaction may also change the image. An extensive experience is required to interpret these variations, and has not been tested in a scientific manner.

In spite of this, experts in court have persuaded themselves that they are absolutely certain that the defendant caused the bite. This cannot be so. There are enormous technical limitations on interpretation which are difficult to express in detail to the jury. In only a small percentage of cases are the details of a bite so clearly demonstrable that it would be safe to conclude that the defendant was responsible (Figure 4). Even in these circumstances, there is a world of difference between a position of 'certainty' and one of 'without reasonable doubt'.

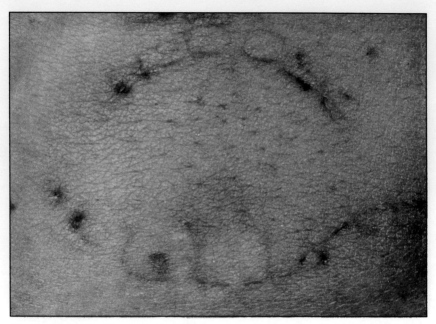

Fig 4. *Bite marks. These may be diffuse or may show details of individual teeth (as in this case).*

Limitations in court

Limitations of communication (Figure 5)

The interface between the expert and the court is often felt to place considerable limitations on the interpretation of the expert's opinions. He may leave the court feeling that communication with his barrister has been less than ideal. Some barristers will seek conference with the expert prior to his appearing in the witness box, but most do not and the expert may never have met his barrister before. How can he communicate in a direct way? How can he present himself in the best possible light in these circumstances? Should there always be some kind of pre-trial meeting and, if so, should it be a formal event? Some barristers will inform experts that they are unable to do this within the law, while others of considerable repute may discuss with the expert for many hours before the trial. Clearly, one of these positions is incorrect.

There are limitations on the expert's ability to choose the right words to convey his meaning, and here he may be aided or obstructed by his barrister. He can never say 'I am one hundred per cent certain' — but what can he say? Can he use terms like 'compatible

LIMITATIONS OF COMMUNICATION

- **With barrister**
- **Pre trial**
- **Limit of report or statement**
- **? pre trial conference**

Fig 5. *Limitations of communication. Relationships between advocate and expert may be important.*

with' or 'commensurate with' and, if so, what do they mean? The expert may know what they mean to *him*, but of course they may not mean the same to the court because they are not absolute terms.

There are additional limitations of communication in court. Bite marks may be highly complicated in a technical sense and require equipment to demonstrate them. The defence may have re-examined the bites and used different methodology and has not communicated this to the prosecution expert or vice versa. How far can the expert resist the temptation to comment on this material or these opinions without having viewed them in detail prior to the trial? What is the law in relation to this particular problem, and how frequently is it flouted?

If the expert feels that in either examination-in-chief or cross-examination the relevant information has not been extracted from him, how far can he go beyond the questions he is asked? Many experts will have experienced a situation in which they have extended their answer beyond the direct question asked, only to be told that their approach is inadmissible and potentially may abort the trial. Other experts have gone ahead and asked the judge if they may comment further and have received an affirmative answer. If, after giving evidence, the expert feels that he has presented the case inadequately, should he go back to his solicitor? Is it then too late

LIMITATIONS OF PERSONALITY

Long experience   **Result**

Careful opinion   **Reject**

Unconvincing witness

                    Short experience   **Result**

                    Unsafe opinion   **Accept**

                    Forceful witness

Fig 6. *Limitations of personality. Experts may influence juries by the manner in which they deliver testimony.*

and has the point been lost? Have experts ever been recalled in these circumstances? All experts have had the experience of, for example, preparing material for overhead projection in court to demonstrate difficult technical points — only to find that the court has failed to provide the necessary equipment. What should the expert do in these circumstances if his counsel wishes to continue regardless?

Limitations of personality (Figure 6)

Finally, there are personality problems. At one end of the spectrum is the expert with many years of long and careful experience, who may appear to the jury as a hesitant, conservative witness, who fails to give a positive and clear opinion simply because he understands the limitations of knowledge. At the other end is the young, keen, newly qualified individual who may present unsafe opinions but who is forceful and clear. The fact that he is wrong is irrelevant. It is difficult to know whether this situation is acceptable because the deliberations of the jury are never revealed. In the ideal situation, where both prosecution and defence counsels understand the issues, the matter may resolve itself under cross-examination in court — but most experts have experienced situations where this is not the case.

Possible solutions

Those then are some of the limitations. What are the possible solutions? There is always a degree of agreement between both prosecution and defence in so far as expert opinion is concerned. This mutual understanding can become blurred by the theatrical activities in court. Pre-trial conferences should always be held, even though they be short and minimal. A closer relationship between prosecution and defence may save time and prevent misunderstandings.

Some of the technicalities within the expert's field may be extremely difficult to debate and present to a lay audience. An agreed position between the experts, allowing the court to debate the areas of doubt or disagreement at the periphery, would seem to offer the best solution.

This combination of inquisitorial and adversarial activity may present problems to the barristers, but may well serve to reduce the many limitations currently influencing the delivery of expert evidence.

PART 3

TRAINING AND QUALITY ASSURANCE

8 Training the medical witness

David J Gee
Emeritus Professor of Forensic Medicine, University of Leeds

In the seven years since I last gave a paper on the topic of training the medical expert witness there has been increased interest in some branches of medicine in this subject — urged on, I suspect, by a greater incidence of legal cases involving patients — but I think much still needs to be done.

Experience of being an expert medical witness

Looking back over the 30-odd years when, as a pathologist, I was engaged in giving evidence in various forms, I realise uncomfortably how little I ever knew of the theory or needs of evidence, or about the responsibilities of giving it. I also realise how little opportunity there was for me to learn. No one ever gave me any formal instruction on the subject of being a witness, little was written about it — one small book[1] (with rather more of it devoted to the collection of evidence than to its presentation), and a brief chapter in some textbooks of forensic medicine. I was lucky — at least in my discipline such written advice, albeit brief, was available. I do not recall any such chapters in books on other specialties.

Any oral advice I received from more experienced medical witnesses was brief, not very profound, and consisted of not trusting the lawyers an inch, especially those on the other side, only answering just what you were asked, and not volunteering any other information, because that might open a chink for the opposition's weapons, or dig a pit for you to fall into.

However, I and my contemporaries had one advantage nowadays denied to pathologists, in that we were able to go to court frequently at a relatively minor level, to inquests and committals. In this way, we were able to become accustomed to the feel of a court and to learn some of the more obvious mistakes that could be made, at a time when such mistakes were more easily rectified, before being exposed to the full glare of publicity in the higher courts. We could learn, in the rather overworked cliché, 'by trial and error'.

It is different now. I heard recently of a senior registrar in pathology, an MRCPath and soon to be a consultant, who had just had his first coroner's court appearance — fortunately having come under the supervision of consultants well aware of the need for such experience. Colleagues have told me that they go to such courts infrequently, and usually only to difficult cases. Even with crown courts, I am told, the tendency is to use written reports, and for medical witnesses to be called only in especially difficult cases (although a crown court judge to whom I spoke did not feel that this was so).

To return to my reminiscing, I realise now that as I made my journey through the various courts I was like a man wandering in a fog, avoiding hazards at the last minute as they loomed up before me, and unaware of the chasms all around. With the words of advice about not trusting the lawyers ringing in my ears, my route was more like an obstacle race than a journey — and, in truth, the actions of some lawyers in those days did little to dispel such a view. Springing the surprise ambush, preventing any communication with or even knowledge of the professional witnesses for the other side, and the absence or minimal nature of any conference even with one's own lawyers, let alone the opposition, did nothing to dispel one's suspicions. Notwithstanding this unhelpful atmosphere, on looking back, I do not think I made too many errors; if this is so, and not just wishful thinking, it is much more by luck than judgment.

Risks inherent in the legal process for the expert witness

In those days, I did not understand the real sources of risk in the legal procedure. It seemed to me that it was a matter of making sure that I was not factually incorrect and of not providing the opposition with any ammunition with which to shoot me down. I now realise, however, that there are certain specific areas of risk inherent in the legal process of which I began to become aware only after I had been acting as an expert witness for a long time. This is borne out by various published studies of miscarriages of justice and their causes.

The principal areas of risk can, I think, be summarised as partisanship, disclosure, competence and relevance. I suspect that all of us have fallen into one or other of these traps at some time in our professional careers.

Partisanship

Partisanship is difficult to avoid, particularly if you do not know that it is a risk. In the usual legal format of confrontation, it certainly may be difficult to adopt anything but a partisan point of view regarding yourself as part of a 'side'. Yet such a stance means that you are unlikely to consider, let alone concede, any points which may be advantageous to the opposition. I know that we all pay lip service to the view that we go to court to assist the court in its deliberations, not any particular 'side', but in practice is this what we *really* do, and do the lawyers *really* want us to?

Disclosure

Such an attitude of partisanship is liable to lead easily into the next problem. Inadequate disclosure seems to have been the source of more miscarriages of justice than any other matter. Yet it was only really in the aftermath of the Clift affair[2] that professional witnesses became more aware of what their responsibilities in this area were considered to be:

> ... (he) shall give his evidence to the best of his ability on his special subject, making a full and frank disclosure so as to provide the court with the material necessary to enable it to come to a reasoned decision on the merits of the scientific issue.[3]

These responsibilities are rather daunting. On the one hand, if you keep any relevant facts to yourself and do not inform the court of them, you are misleading it — but how do you know *what* facts are relevant? Of course, the problem can be solved by telling the court absolutely everything, and letting it decide what is relevant — but it is unlikely to thank you for doing so. A nice judgment, or good luck, is required to avoid this hazard.

Also, witnesses may be led astray by lines of questioning by lawyers, and fail to make adequate disclosure as a result. The lawyer is aiming at a particular outcome, and in any case he does not know all the information possessed by the doctor. I used to think that this was likely to happen only in the higher courts, but colleagues have told me recently that they have occasionally encountered this problem with coroners, some of whom let you make your report unhindered, while others, perhaps less experienced, use a particular line of leading questions.

Competence

Competence may be considered to have two heads: first, competence in one's discipline, being a good doctor of whatever variety.
Fortunately, not many doctors are incompetent under this first
heading, though of course they may be inexperienced.

Secondly, competence in giving evidence, which may be acquired
either from experience or by instruction. A problem about incompetence under this heading is that the only real criterion for determining it lies in the discovery of miscarriages of justice — otherwise,
even though one 'does it wrong', no one will know.

Relevance

Finally, relevance. In most respects, this relates to disclosure. Unless
the evidence you are giving is relevant to what the court is trying to
decide, it is useless and you are wasting everyone's time. Unless you
understand the procedures of the court in relation to evidence, and
how the law of evidence works, you are unlikely to appreciate this.

Problems like these give some indication of the fallibility of oral
witnesses — quite apart from downright perjury. It indicates why
over the centuries the courts have been loath to accept oral evidence if anything else is available, for example, documents, and why
other sources of information were used at different times, for example, the ordeal or the early medieval jury. Just because we are superior to our predecessors in scientific knowledge does not make us
any less fallible in the peculiar environment of the court.

The importance of training expert witnesses

We are likely to say 'Ah well, competence will come with experience', but I am reminded of Oscar Wilde's comment that
'Experience was ... merely the name men gave to their mistakes'.[4]
Such mistakes can hurt us, and much more so the recipient of a
wrong decision by the court. Clearly, the number of such mistakes
needs to be reduced for everyone's sake. The way to do this, surely,
is by training the potential witness for his role. After all, lawyers have
always been trained to deal with witnesses, and to extract from them
the evidence they require. There are books written on the subject,
and instructions given. Consider some of the chapter heads in one
such book:[5] 'Cross-examination of medical witnesses', 'Impeaching
the reliability of witnesses' and 'Attacking prosecution witnesses'. If
the lawyers can be so well trained for their role, why not medical
witnesses?

One difficulty, I feel, is the attitude of medicine, that its forensic aspect is not a subject worthy of study in its own right, that it is merely something that will happen automatically, like sex, and all that is necessary is for the doctor to answer truthfully and accurately questions put to him. Of course, too, lawyers are keen to suggest that it is wrong to prepare a witness, that he should arrive at his questioning pure and unadulterated. This must be correct for a witness purely to *fact*. No such witness should be coached for his role. But we are talking about professional or expert witnesses, from whom clearly the court expects a special standard of evidence — and says so, for example in a recent *Times Law Report*:[6]

> ... the expert who advanced such a hypothesis owed a very heavy
> duty to explain to the court that what he was advancing was a
> hypothesis, that it was controversial, if it was, and to place before
> the court all the material which contradicted the hypothesis.

The legal profession cannot have it both ways. If it wants to have medical witnesses who know exactly what is required of them, and who are able to avoid the pitfalls of such matters as incomplete disclosure, it cannot also expect to have 'virgin' witnesses unsullied by any knowledge of legal proceedings. Lawyers would not be happy to have their stomachs removed by a doctor innocent of any surgical training! So surely we should train doctors to perform their role as professional witnesses adequately.

Of what should the training consist?

How should this be done? In the first place, it is clear that most doctors will probably go to court only a few times in the course of their professional careers, though of course they may have to prepare reports more often. It would therefore be foolish to provide extensive training for most practitioners, but at least they should have available to them sources of information on which to draw if it becomes necessary.

There may not be much point in further burdening an already overcrowded undergraduate curriculum, where teaching of forensic medicine is now virtually extinct, but all doctors now have postgraduate training in some form or other. This would be the most sensible place, not least because by that time the doctor would have sufficient experience of his discipline to understand the relevance and difficulties of conveying information to others. At the very least, the importance of clinical notes, and the fact that bad or inadequate ones may lead to legal problems later, should be emphasised.

Doctors in certain disciplines are more likely than most to be involved in legal proceedings: neurologists, psychiatrists, accident and emergency surgeons, paediatricians, histopathologists, and so forth. They need more extensive instruction, which they are getting in some disciplines such as psychiatry, though I am bound to say that I do not think this is so in pathology.

As will be clear from what I have already said, I feel that the emphasis nowadays has shifted from court-room appearances towards evidence given by report, so an understanding of both the importance of a good report in the evolution of legal events and also in the form of any subsequent court appearances needs to be instilled in all doctors.

Training in legal procedures

I suspect, though, that even in disciplines given extensive training, it is done only from the medical point of view. An experienced clinical colleague confessed to feeling baffled still by the legal procedure, and said that his overriding concern was for his patient. We could not disagree with that view, but the court also has a need, for a time, as great as that of the patient. As a pathologist, I usually felt that the court was my patient.

I feel therefore that there is a requirement in such training for much greater exploration of the areas I have already touched on briefly. To learn how to prepare these reports requires the cooperation of lawyers, both to interpret their philosophy of the law of evidence and, more practically, to explain what the court needs and how it needs it. Young doctors must know of the hazards of disclosure, and the ease with which a partisan role can be adopted, and what may result. They also need to know about the lawyer's techniques, so that in the witness box they can avoid being 'persuaded' into giving evidence to the court which may mislead it, although it may benefit the lawyer's client. In forensic pathology, the Policy Advisory Board for Forensic Pathology (Chapter 9) has made a start along these lines.

Ideally, doctors should have some experience of the sensation of being in a witness box and of being cross-examined. Other disciplines often do this, though I feel pathology should do much better — perhaps with help from the Coroners' Society. There are plenty of examples of how other professions provide this sort of training, for example, the Forensic Science Service, the Institute of Advanced Legal Studies and the British Academy of Experts (which organises practical court-room experience). In days gone by, when I was teaching medical students, in addition to lectures we would take them to sit in the back of a court in session to watch and hear the proceedings. I have never found anyone experiencing a court for the first time who did not find it daunting and instructive — even if, in the end, he decided that the whole process was a nonsense.

The *British Medical Journal* sponsored a course in November 1994 provided by a professional firm, giving training along the lines I have already suggested. I hope that it was successful.

Conclusion

In all this, notwithstanding Oscar Wilde, nothing can really replace the role of experience: there is no alternative to being responsible for a case, to being in a real court with its smell and its bustle, and feeling the loneliness of the witness box. We must do all we can to prepare the potential witness so that he makes the best use of his experience when he gets it, especially as nowadays it may well be in a difficult case, and his first court experience might be his last.

References

1. Simpson K. *A doctor's guide to court*. London: Butterworths, 1962.
2. Brownlie AR. Expert evidence in the light of Preece v. HM Advocate. *Medicine, Science and the Law* 1982;**22**:237–44.
3. *Davie v. Edinburgh magistrates* [1953] SC 34, SLT 54 (SCOT).
4. Wilde O. *The picture of Dorian Gray*. London: Ward, Lock & Co, 1891.
5. Napley Sir D. *The technique of persuasion*, 3rd edn. London: Sweet & Maxwell, 1983.
6. *Re AB (a minor)* (medical issues: expert evidence) [1994] TLR, 17 Aug.

9

The role of the Policy Advisory Board for Forensic Pathology

Trevor J Rothwell
Secretary, Home Office Policy Advisory Board for Forensic Pathology

Whenever expert evidence is to be presented, the primary consideration must be the quality of the work which is done. The manner in which the Home Office Policy Advisory Board for Forensic Pathology operates to monitor and develop the specialty of forensic pathology in England and Wales, and thus to raise the standards of expert evidence provided for the courts, will be considered in this chapter.

The forensic pathologist

The task of the forensic pathologist is to examine the body and, if necessary, the scene of the incident, to ascertain the cause of any death which occurs suddenly or in suspicious circumstances. The approach of the forensic pathologist broadly parallels that of the forensic scientist. It involves ascertaining facts from the various elements of the examination, whether conducted at the scene or at the autopsy itself. To maximise the value of the practitioner's work to the investigator and ultimately to the courts, the observed facts must be interpreted in the light of the available information. This interpretation is designed to assist the coroner to understand the reasons for the death, and the police investigator to learn more of the course of events which may have taken place during the commission of a crime.

The results of any work undertaken by the pathologist may become an important part of a police investigation. The ultimate goal of the forensic pathologist's work is the preparation of a report which will become part of the evidence at an inquest or to some other court in the civil or criminal justice system. In work of this nature it is vital that the quality of all aspects of the service provided is above reproach.

The expert in court

All those who regularly appear in the courts are judged by the way in which they perform in the witness box. In this environment, the witness will be asked questions designed to test both his knowledge and his strength of conviction. Several different interpretations of the nature and effects of, say, injuries observed at post-mortem may be put to the expert during cross-examination. Those who express and maintain firm opinions under such questioning may acquire reputations as good witnesses. This is not surprising: the lawyers conducting the case will know exactly where they stand when the expert appears unshakeable. The jury, where present, may also gain a favourable impression of the expert as an individual who knows the subject so well as to be quite sure where he stands on the issue in question. It is also undoubtedly important that the expert witness should express his opinions in a straightforward, clear and confident manner.

While such confidence in a witness may be entirely justified, it can also be misplaced. The pathologist's report which forms the basis of the evidence will have been drawn up on the best information available to the practitioner at the time. Developments in the investigation subsequent to the preparation of the pathologist's report could mean, for instance, that one of the lawyers may be able to put to the pathologist in the witness box a completely different scenario concerning the causation of certain injuries found on a body. In such circumstances, the effective expert should not refuse to accept any different explanation for the facts, but should be able to assimilate the new information and react to it in a positive fashion, weighing up the possible explanations for his findings and attempting to offer the most rational interpretation. In some instances, the pathologist may have to ask for more time to take a considered view of the new situation. Scientifically and ethically, this is the right decision, although to the court it can appear as vacillation or a lack of self confidence on the part of the witness.

The assessment of quality

Forensic pathology as practised in England and Wales is of a high quality, and its practitioners offer a professional service to the coroners and police officers whom they serve. No profession can rest on its laurels, however, and monitoring the standard of work to ensure the maintenance of high standards is one of the functions of a professional body. Any assessment of quality must concern itself with every aspect of the pathologist's work, from the initial examination at the scene of the incident, through the details of the autopsy and preparation of the report of the examination, to the manner in which the individual performs in court.

The standard of the work performed by the forensic pathologist, in common with that of many other experts who serve the criminal justice system, may not be immediately apparent to the user of the practitioner's services. If asked, both the coroner and the police officer would be absolutely genuine in giving 'the quality of the work' as their highest priority. However, their primary task is to seek the answers to specific questions. For the coroner, these questions will be concerned with the immediate cause of death, while the police officer's concerns are likely to focus on the collection of information which will assist in the apprehension of an offender.

It may not, in fact, be possible for either the coroner or the police officer properly to judge whether appropriate standards are being adhered to by the pathologist employed to assist during an investigation. In saying this, I do not in any way detract from the experience, intelligence or perceptiveness of the coroner or police officer, but simply mean that these individuals may be in no position to assess quality. The pathologist may be dealing with matters outside the experience of even a medically qualified coroner — and, apart from London, most coroners tend to be legal rather than medical practitioners. As customer satisfaction appears to be a less than adequate guide to quality, it is vital to call on the various procedures of audit and peer review when attempting to judge the standard to which practitioners are working.

The Home Office Policy Advisory Board for Forensic Pathology

It may be useful to give a brief outline of the history and function of the Policy Advisory Board for Forensic Pathology before describing how it attempts to influence the profession of forensic pathology. The Home Office has a central role within the criminal justice system, particularly in the provision of technical support for the police. In 1984, the then Home Secretary initiated the formation of a working party under the chairmanship of Mr G J Wassermann, head of the Home Office Police Department Science and Technology Group, to examine the state of forensic pathology within England and Wales. The group comprised senior members of the profession and representatives of other interested bodies such as the Association of Chief Police Officers, the Crown Prosecution Service, the Coroners' Society, and the Department of Health.

It was generally accepted at that time that forensic pathology as a specialty was in decline, with the subject being dropped from the curriculum of many medical schools. This had led to the running down of academic departments and, to some extent, the loss of status of the specialty and its practitioners. It was also clear, however, that the subject continued to be of the highest importance in the investigation of major crime.

The working party reported in 1989,[1] and in due course the Policy Advisory Board for Forensic Pathology was created, with a membership similar to that of the working party. Its terms of reference include the creation and maintenance of a Home Office register of properly trained and accredited practitioners, and the initiation of effective quality assurance programmes to monitor and improve scientific standards. In its various ways the Advisory Board complements the activities of the Royal College of Pathologists and of the General Medical Council, while not subverting the actions of either body.

Role of the Advisory Board

The Advisory Board seeks to maintain and improve the standards of forensic pathology in England and Wales, first, by attempting to ensure that only properly qualified and experienced doctors are appointed to the register and, secondly, through the operation of quality assurance and training programmes to monitor the output and promote the development of registered practitioners. It needs to be pointed out, however, that the activities of the Board are still at a relatively early stage, and time will tell how effective the various initiatives prove to be in practice.

Accreditation

In order to gain Home Office accreditation the forensic pathologist must hold necessary qualifications such as the Diploma in Medical Jurisprudence or specialist membership of the Royal College of Pathologists. He will also have spent time, typically at least six months, working in a recognised department of forensic medicine. The initial appointment to the Home Office register of forensic pathologists is for a period of up to two years, during which time the first review of the practitioner's work will be undertaken.

The quality assurance programme

Audit

An important element of the quality assurance programme involves the audit of practitioners' work on a regular basis. This is achieved through the examination of case reports produced by Home Office registered forensic pathologists, obtained through the cooperation of the Crown Prosecution Service. This method of obtaining reports ensures that the material subjected to scrutiny is actually that which has been used by the prosecution in the construction of the file of evidence for court — it has been revealed that errors can be generated during the retyping of a pathologist's original report. Feedback on performance is provided individually to pathologists at the completion of the audit. The first audit was completed at the end of 1994, and this is expected to be the first exercise in a rolling programme.

Review

The review procedure provides an opportunity for the users of forensic pathology services to offer their views. While customer satisfaction may not necessarily be the best indicator of professional standards, important issues are the pathologist being available at the time and place expected, delivering reports on time, and being prepared to explain the technical details. These all bear heavily on the value of the service as perceived by the police officer, and similar issues are important in the context of the court. Following the first review of a forensic pathologist's work, which is carried out within two years of accreditation, reviews are conducted five yearly. The outcome of each review must be successful if the practitioner is to retain accreditation.

Training and research

Training

Adequate standards can be promoted and maintained only when individuals are properly trained for the task. Prior to making an application for accreditation, a pathologist may, where appropriate, receive training through attachment to a department of forensic medicine. It is possible to obtain financial assistance from the Advisory Board if necessary, for instance, to secure the services of a locum to cover for the pathologist during this period of attachment.

The Advisory Board also arranges seminars on relevant subjects. These are open to all, but as an inducement registered practitioners are usually invited to attend at no cost to themselves. It is hoped that meetings and courses sponsored by the Advisory Board will eventually integrate with other continuing professional development programmes.

Research

Research can also raise standards through the introduction of new procedures and techniques, and the Home Office is able to support a limited programme of research in the specialty.

The development of the profession

A major stimulus behind the creation of the Home Office working party and the subsequent formation of the Advisory Board was the decline of the specialty as an academic discipline. As part of the attempt to reverse this decline, funding has been provided by the Home Office to enable a small number of senior posts to be created in departments of forensic medicine.

Conclusion

This chapter has highlighted the role of the forensic pathologist and offered some comment on the way in which an individual who provides expert evidence to the courts needs to operate. It has also described the work of the Home Office Policy Advisory Board for Forensic Pathology in accrediting and appointing practitioners to the Home Office register, in monitoring the work of the specialty and in promoting its development. There are signs that these initiatives are indeed helping to raise the profile of the profession and assisting it to offer an even better service to the coroners and the courts.

Reference

1. Home Office. *Report of the working party on forensic pathology*. London: HMSO, 1989.

10 Overview

Bernard Knight
Professor of Forensic Pathology

Stephen Leadbeatter
Senior Lecturer in Forensic Pathology

Wales Institute of Forensic Medicine, University of Wales College of Medicine, Institute of Pathology, Cardiff Royal Infirmary

The papers and ensuing discussions demonstrated clearly the uncertainty felt by individual expert witnesses at both the apparent lack of clear-cut legal guidance regarding their role and the diversity of any legal guidance or opinion from counsel in different cases. This extended to such mundane issues as what matters relating to the case may be discussed with whom when the witness is 'part heard', and what prosecution and defence witnesses may discuss when both are present at an examination. All agreed that the term 'expert witness' should refer to a witness who is an expert in the field at issue in the case and not to an individual who is merely expert at being a witness. There was some concern, however, that at least experience, if not expertise, in being a witness was necessary to ensure that evidence which the expert witness considered relevant to the case was brought out in examination-in-chief or in cross-examination. It reflects badly on the degree of mutual understanding between the legal and medical/scientific communities if it is indeed the case that lawyers fear that doctors will not recognise that certain forms of evidence are inadmissible or that the latter fear that the former are not concerned with eliciting all the evidence.

Of fundamental importance was clear direction from Judge Stephens that the rule that a barrister is not allowed to have a conference with a witness does not apply to expert witnesses. We agree wholeheartedly that expert witnesses should always have a conference with counsel, and feel that early conference between police, experts, Crown Prosecution Service and, if practicable, counsel is of fundamental importance both to an investigation and to any later criminal proceedings. Such a conference would define the basic background events of a case, so that the expert's opinion from the

83

objective evidence may then be set in context and indicate further lines of investigation which might clarify potential issues or discrepancies. From the legal point of view, this early conference would demonstrate the solidity and admissibility of the basis for the expert's opinion.

It is of interest that the tenor of the papers by Drs Eastman, Leadbeatter and Whittaker (the first pair of whom cannot be accused of collusion!) was not discordant. Experts should demonstrate the basis of their opinions, remembering both that it is not yet universal for a defendant to have access to an independent expert and also that, even were it so, it would be unethical to leave testing of the strength of poorly-based opinion dependent upon the ability of defence counsel to identify and explore such weaknesses. Again, if personal observation and knowledge of the literature do not allow the expert to give a firm opinion, he should acknowledge his inability to do so, and demonstrate to the jury, for their judgment, the current parameters of argument within his field.

It is heartening that the Policy Advisory Board for Forensic Pathology has begun a process of accreditation or quality control, at least in so far as the technical adequacy of a post-mortem examination is concerned, but this exercise must be consolidated and extended to scrutiny of the opinion based upon that examination. Such stringent peer review would appear to be the solution to the question regarding the assessment of competence of those presenting themselves as experts to a court. A person's listing in a register maintained by the relevant peer group should go far to guard against a failure to demonstrate the incompetence of a self-styled 'expert' and the waste of court time (and public money) that such a successful demonstration might entail. Neither the legal nor medical/scientific communities appears to favour the system, seen in some European countries, of 'court-appointed experts'.[1]

Much discussion centred around pre-trial disclosure and the apparent ineffectiveness of the Crown Court (Advance Notice of Expert Evidence) Rules 1987. Dr Whittaker had been exposed on more than one occasion to expert evidence brought by the defence only at trial, so that his opportunity to examine and comment upon that material was limited. Admittedly, this might represent only a failure of the prosecution lawyers to realise the significance of the material when disclosed in advance and their failure to bring it to the attention of their expert. It is obvious that were there to be a pre-trial conference between prosecution lawyers and experts at an appropriate interval before trial — not, as it were, 'at the door of the court' — such a situation would be avoided. There is a strong current of opinion among expert witnesses that there should be a move to formal pre-trial discussion. This would go far to identifying true 'points of issue' between experts, upon which questioning could be focused at trial and those cases where there was no issue, so that court time and public money (and, perhaps not least, the experts' own time) might be saved by not requiring oral evidence from the experts. Were such pre-trial discussion to be formalised, as appears to be the case in the civil courts,[2] it would relieve the atmosphere of constraint felt by some experts at examinations in the presence of 'a player on the other side' as to what comments or questions are permissible regarding the findings at earlier examination and what further examinations might be required.

There was judicial sympathy for the ethical disquiet felt by the expert when an opinion sought by the defence was not used and that expert was then summoned as a witness by the prosecution, but it was emphasised that, if called upon to answer a question in the witness box, the expert has no privilege and must answer that question even should the answer breach 'medical confidentiality'. Of course, if an opinion prepared for the defence is sought by the prosecution in any other way, the expert will refuse to disclose that opinion without the consent of the instructing solicitors.

In summary, therefore, both lawyers and experts should communicate more freely and frequently, directing their attention to:

- assessment of competence of those who claim expertise;

- continuing assessment of the quality of expert opinion and the basis upon which it is founded (these first two areas are both best addressed by peer review);

- clarification of how best to address issues upon which expert opinion may be adduced (an area where we would welcome greater use of pre-trial conferences between lawyers and experts); and

- a method of training for giving expert evidence superior to 'trial and error' acquisition of experience in real cases.

Only by cooperation and action in these areas can lawyers and experts better serve the ends of justice, rather than what may appear to be the artificial constraints of the adversarial system or their own convenience.

References

1. Hodgkinson T. *Expert evidence: law and practice.* London: Sweet & Maxwell, 1990.
2. *RSC (Amendment no. 2)* 1986 (SI 1986 no. 1187).